STEM Integration in K–12 Education

STATUS, PROSPECTS, AND AN AGENDA FOR RESEARCH

Committee on Integrated STEM Education

Margaret Honey, Greg Pearson, and Heidi Schweingruber, *Editors*

NATIONAL ACADEMY OF ENGINEERING *AND*
NATIONAL RESEARCH COUNCIL
OF THE NATIONAL ACADEMIES

THE NATIONAL ACADEMIES PRESS
Washington, D.C.
www.nap.edu

THE NATIONAL ACADEMIES PRESS   500 Fifth Street, NW   Washington, DC 20001

NOTICE: The project that is the subject of this report was approved by the Governing Board of the National Research Council, whose members are drawn from the councils of the National Academy of Sciences, the National Academy of Engineering, and the Institute of Medicine. The members of the committee responsible for the report were chosen for their special competences and with regard for appropriate balance.

This study was supported by a grant between the National Academy of Sciences and S.D. Bechtel, Jr. Foundation and Stephen Bechtel Fund. Additional support was provided by the National Science Foundation (Contract/Grant No. DRL-1114829), Samueli Foundation, and PTC, Inc. Any opinions, findings, conclusions, or recommendations expressed in this publication are those of the author(s) and do not necessarily reflect the views of the organizations or agencies that provided support for the project.

International Standard Book Number-13:   978-0-309-29796-7
International Standard Book Number-10:   0-309-29796-6
Library of Congress Control Number: 2014931444

Copies of this report are available from the National Academies Press, 500 Fifth Street, NW, Keck 360, Washington, DC 20001; (800) 624-6242 or (202) 334-3313; www.nap.edu.

THE NATIONAL ACADEMIES
Advisers to the Nation on Science, Engineering, and Medicine

The **National Academy of Sciences** is a private, nonprofit, self-perpetuating society of distinguished scholars engaged in scientific and engineering research, dedicated to the furtherance of science and technology and to their use for the general welfare. Upon the authority of the charter granted to it by the Congress in 1863, the Academy has a mandate that requires it to advise the federal government on scientific and technical matters. Dr. Ralph J. Cicerone is president of the National Academy of Sciences.

The **National Academy of Engineering** was established in 1964, under the charter of the National Academy of Sciences, as a parallel organization of outstanding engineers. It is autonomous in its administration and in the selection of its members, sharing with the National Academy of Sciences the responsibility for advising the federal government. The National Academy of Engineering also sponsors engineering programs aimed at meeting national needs, encourages education and research, and recognizes the superior achievements of engineers. Dr. C. D. Mote, Jr., is president of the National Academy of Engineering.

The **Institute of Medicine** was established in 1970 by the National Academy of Sciences to secure the services of eminent members of appropriate professions in the examination of policy matters pertaining to the health of the public. The Institute acts under the responsibility given to the National Academy of Sciences by its congressional charter to be an adviser to the federal government and, upon its own initiative, to identify issues of medical care, research, and education. Dr. Harvey V. Fineberg is president of the Institute of Medicine.

The **National Research Council** was organized by the National Academy of Sciences in 1916 to associate the broad community of science and technology with the Academy's purposes of furthering knowledge and advising the federal government. Functioning in accordance with general policies determined by the Academy, the Council has become the principal operating agency of both the National Academy of Sciences and the National Academy of Engineering in providing services to the government, the public, and the scientific and engineering communities. The Council is administered jointly by both Academies and the Institute of Medicine. Dr. Ralph J. Cicerone and Dr. C. D. Mote, Jr., are chair and vice chair, respectively, of the National Research Council.

www.national-academies.org

COMMITTEE ON INTEGRATED STEM EDUCATION

MARGARET A. HONEY (*chair*), New York Hall of Science, Queens
LINDA ABRIOLA, Tufts University, Medford, Massachusetts
SYBILLA BECKMANN, University of Georgia, Athens
SUSAN HACKWOOD, California Council on Science and Technology, Riverside
ALFRED L. HALL II, The University of Memphis, Tennessee
JENNIFER HICKS, Purdue University, West Lafayette, Indiana
STEVE KRAK, Ohio STEM Learning Network Battelle, Columbus
BILL KURTZ, DSST Public Schools, Denver, Colorado
RICHARD LEHRER, Vanderbilt University, Nashville, Tennessee
BETH MCGRATH, Stevens Institute of Technology, Hoboken, New Jersey
BARBARA MEANS, SRI International, Menlo Park, California
DONNA MIGDOL, Oceanside School District, New York
MITCHELL NATHAN, University of Wisconsin, Madison
MARK SANDERS, Virginia Polytechnic Institute and State University, Blacksburg
MICHAEL TOWN, Redmond High School, Duvall, Washington

Project Staff

GREG PEARSON, Study Director and Senior Program Officer, National Academy of Engineering
HEIDI SCHWEINGRUBER, Study Codirector and Deputy Board Director, Board on Science Education, National Research Council
JAY LABOV, Senior Advisor for Education and Communication, The National Academies
CAMERON H. FLETCHER, Senior Editor, National Academy of Engineering
MARIBETH KEITZ, Senior Program Associate, National Academy of Engineering
REBECCA KRONE, Project Associate, Board on Science Education, National Research Council

Preface

This report is the final product of a two-year study by the Committee on Integrated STEM Education, a group of experts on diverse subjects under the auspices of the National Academy of Engineering (NAE) and the Board on Science Education of the National Research Council (NRC). The committee's charge was to develop a research agenda for determining the approaches and conditions most likely to lead to positive outcomes of integrated STEM (science, technology, engineering, mathematics) education at the K–12 level in the United States. In fulfilling that charge, the committee identified and characterized existing approaches to integrated STEM education, in both formal and after-school and informal settings. It also reviewed the evidence for the impact of integrated approaches on various parameters of interest, such as greater student awareness, interest, motivation, and achievement in STEM subjects; improved college-readiness skills; and boosts in the number and quality of students who may consider a career in a STEM-related field.

Over the past decade, the STEM acronym has developed wide currency in US education and policy circles. Leaders in business, government, and academia assert that education in the STEM subjects is vital not only to sustaining the innovation capacity of the United States but also as a foundation for successful employment, including but not limited to work in the STEM fields. Historically, US K–12 STEM education has focused on the individual subjects, particularly science and mathematics. Reform efforts, including development of learning standards and, more recently, large-scale assessments, likewise have treated the STEM subjects mostly in isolation. The relatively recent introduction of engineering education into some K–12 classrooms and out-of-school settings and the 2013 publication of the *Next Generation Science Standards,* which explicitly connect science concepts and practices to those of engineering, have elevated the idea of integration as a potential component of STEM education. Recognizing that education within the individual STEM disciplines has great value and that efforts to improve discipline-centered teaching and learning should continue, this project considers the potential benefits—and challenges—of an explicit focus on integration.

The report's primary audience is education researchers and those working in the cognitive and learning sciences. It is these individuals to whom the committee's research agenda is directed. However, the report contains much more than the agenda. It should also prove useful to the large, diverse set of individuals directly involved in or supportive of efforts to improve STEM education in the United States. These include educators, school leaders, curriculum and assessment developers, and those engaged in teacher education and professional development, as well as policymakers and employers.

The committee met five times, sponsored three data-gathering workshops, commissioned several reviews of the relevant research, and studied a subset of programs and projects judged to be engaged in some form of integrated STEM education. Beyond this data gathering, the report reflects the personal and professional experiences and judgments of committee members.

Although our report falls far short of an unequivocal endorsement of integrated approaches to STEM education, I know I speak for my committee colleagues in noting the exciting potential of leveraging the natural connections between and among the four STEM subjects for the benefit of students.

Margaret A. Honey, *Chair*

Acknowledgments

This report has been reviewed in draft form by individuals chosen for their diverse perspectives and technical expertise, in accordance with procedures approved by the NRC's Report Review Committee. The purpose of this independent review is to provide candid and critical comments that will assist the institution in making its published report as sound as possible and to ensure that the report meets institutional standards for objectivity, evidence, and responsiveness to the study charge. The review comments and draft manuscript remain confidential to protect the integrity of the deliberative process. We wish to thank the following individuals for their review of this report:

Rodger W. Bybee, Executive Director (Retired), Biological Sciences Curriculum Study

David Crismond, Teaching Learning and Culture: Science Education, The City College of New York

L. Berkley Davis, Chief Consulting Engineer, Systems, GE Power Generation Products

Lucille E. Davy, Senior Advisor, The Hunt Institute

Kim Day, Health, Science and Mathematics Branch, The Department of Defense Education Activity

David Heil, David Heil and Associates, Inc., Portland, OR

Mackenzie D. Hird, Engineering Systems Division, Massachusetts Institute of Technology

Marie Hoepfl, Department of Technology and Environmental Design, Appalachian State University

William Hunter, Center for Mathematics, Science, and Technology, Illinois State University

Joseph Krajcik, College of Natural Science and College of Education, University of Michigan

Richard C. Larson, Engineering Systems Division, Massachusetts Institute of Technology

Richard S. Muller, Department of Electrical Engineering and Computer Science, University of California, Berkeley

Anthony Petrosino, Mathematics and Science Education, University of Texas, Austin

Amy Sabarre, PK–12 STEM and PK-5 Science, Harrisonburg City Public Schools, Harrisonburg, VA

Norman H. Sleep, Department of Geophysics, Stanford University

Roberta Tanner, Physics and Physical Science, Loveland High School, Loveland, CO

Although the reviewers listed above provided many constructive comments and suggestions, they were not asked to endorse the conclusions or recommendations nor did they see the final draft of the report before its release. The review of this report was overseen by Lawrence D. Brown, Department of Statistics, The Wharton School, University of Pennsylvania and Carlo Parravano, Executive Director (retired), Merck Institute for Science Education. Appointed by the National Research Council, they were responsible for making certain that an independent examination of this report was carried out in accordance with institutional procedures and that all review comments were carefully considered. Responsibility for the final content of this report rests entirely with the authoring committee and the institution.

In addition to the reviewers, many other individuals assisted in the development of this report. David Heil and Associates, Inc. (DHA) oversaw an ambitious synthesis of literature related to the outcomes of integrated STEM education. DHA received considerable help on this task from Kenneth Welty, University of Wisconsin, Stout, who performed a detailed analysis of the literature related to formal education, from Cary Sneider, Portland State University, who conducted a similar analysis of literature in the informal education arena, and from Eli M. Silk and Christian D. Schunn, University of Pittsburgh, who reviewed the cognitive sciences literature related to integrated STEM education. DHA also prepared summaries of a number of projects or programs engaged in integrated STEM education, and the firm conducted in-depth interviews with individual stakeholders in STEM education on the committee's behalf. Both efforts were important input for committee deliberations.

Inverness Research conducted the project's formative and summative evaluations. The firm prepared detailed summaries, including feedback from participants and Inverness's own observations, of two of the committee's workshops. These documents helped clarify the committee's thinking on a number of points. Inverness will also track impact of the committee report.

The committee benefited greatly from several commissioned papers. Mary Gauvain, University of California, Riverside, prepared a paper on the social context of learning and integrated STEM education; K. Ann Renninger, Swarthmore College, wrote a paper addressing the development of interest in integrated STEM education; Angela Calabrese Barton, Michigan State University, contributed a review of identity research in science education and its implications for integrated STEM education experiences; Edys Quellmalz, WestEd, addressed the issue of assessment of student learning in the context of integrated STEM; and Steven Marc Weisberg, Temple University, explored embodied cognition approaches in integrated STEM education. The committee's report is much richer for these contributions. The committee also wishes to thank the many other experts and practitioners who took the time to attend the project workshops and share their perspectives on integrated STEM education.

Thanks are also due to the project staff. Maribeth Keitz managed the study's logistical and administrative needs, making sure meetings and workshops ran efficiently and smoothly. Christine Mirzayan Science & Technology Policy Graduate Fellow Kristen Coakley did extensive background research on previous efforts to describe STEM education in the United States. NAE Senior Editor Cameron H. Fletcher substantially improved the readability of the report. Greg Pearson, at the NAE, played a key role in conceptualizing the study. He and study codirector Heidi Schweingruber, of the NRC Board on Science Education, ably guided the project from its inception.

Contents

Summary

Education for students in science, technology, engineering, and mathematics (STEM) has received increasing attention over the past decade with calls both for greater emphasis on these fields and for improvements in the quality of curricula and instruction. In response, numerous new instructional materials, programs, and specialized schools are emerging. While most of these initiatives address one or more of the STEM subjects separately, there are increasing calls for emphasizing connections between and among the subjects.

Advocates of more integrated approaches to K–12 STEM education argue that teaching STEM in a more connected manner, especially in the context of real-world issues, can make the STEM subjects more relevant to students and teachers. This in turn can enhance motivation for learning and improve student interest, achievement, and persistence. And these outcomes, advocates assert, will help address calls for greater workplace and college readiness as well as increase the number of students who consider a career in a STEM-related field.

Recently, both the *Common Core State Standards for Mathematics* (CCSSM) and the *Next Generation Science Standards* (NGSS) have called for more and deeper connections among the STEM subjects. The NGSS explicitly includes practices and core disciplinary ideas from engineering alongside those for science, raising the expectation that science teachers will be expected to teach science and engineering in an integrated fashion.

Despite the rise in interest in providing students with learning experiences that foster connection making across the STEM disciplines, there is little research on how best to do so or on what factors make integration more likely to increase student learning, interest, retention, achievement, or other valued outcomes. Recognizing the need for a more robust evidence base, the National Academy of Engineering (NAE) and the Board on Science Education of the National Research Council (NRC) convened a committee to examine current efforts to integrate the STEM disciplines in K–12 education and develop a research agenda that, if carried out, could provide the data needed to inform such efforts going forward.

The NAE/NRC Committee on Integrated STEM Education was charged with

- identifying and characterizing existing approaches to integrated STEM education, both in formal and after-/out-of-school settings,
- reviewing the evidence for the impact of integrated approaches on various student outcomes, and
- determining a set of priority research questions to advance understanding of integrated STEM education.

DESCRIPTIVE FRAMEWORK

Far from being a single, well-defined experience, integrated STEM education includes a range of different experiences that involve some degree of connection. The experiences may occur in one or several class periods, throughout a curriculum, be reflected in the organization of a single course or an entire school, or be encompassed in an out-of-school activity. Each variant of integrated STEM education suggests different planning approaches, resource needs, implementation challenges, and outcomes.

To make sense of this confusing landscape, the committee developed a descriptive framework. The framework is meant to provide a common perspective and vocabulary for researchers, practitioners, and others to identify, discuss, and investigate specific integrated STEM initiatives within the K–12 education system of the United States. Although potentially a very large number of variables could be incorporated into such a framework, the committee chose to focus on four high-level features: goals, outcomes, nature of integration, and implementation.

Goals identified in the framework include building STEM literacy and 21st century competencies; developing a STEM-capable workforce; and boosting interest and engagement in STEM. In terms of outcomes, the framework considers learning and achievement; STEM course taking; STEM-related employment; development of "STEM identity"; and the ability to transfer understanding across STEM disciplines. Regarding the nature and scope of integration, the framework addresses which subjects are connected; which disciplines are dominant; and the duration, size, and complexity of an initiative. With respect to implementation, the framework focuses on instructional designs involving problem-based learning and engineering design; the type of educator supports present, such as pre- and in-service professional development and development of professional learning communities; and adjustments to the learning environment, such as extended class periods, extended lesson planning, team teaching, and partnering between STEM educators working in and outside of schools.

RESEARCH ON THE IMPACTS OF INTEGRATED STEM EDUCATION

In reviewing the literature, the committee focused on research related to the potential impact of integrated STEM education in two areas: learning and achievement, and interest and identity. Looking across studies, the integration of STEM concepts and practices has the promise to lead to increased conceptual learning within the disciplines. However, the positive impact on learning appears to differ for science and mathematics, with less evidence of a positive impact on mathematics outcomes, based on current assessments for those subject areas, which might not fully capture integrated learning in STEM. For both science and mathematics, the impact on learning and achievement depends on the approach to integration and the kinds of supports that are embedded in the experience and provided through instruction. Integrated STEM education also shows promise of supporting knowledge gains in engineering and technology. Given the small number of studies, generally small sample sizes, and reliance on pre- and post-study designs, however, these potentially promising findings must be interpreted cautiously.

There are indications that integrated STEM experiences can support interest development, but research studies vary considerably in quality and often do not take into account the different phases of interest development, limiting what can be concluded from this work. Integrated STEM education experiences may provide opportunities for students to engage in STEM in ways that potentially transform their identities with respect to the STEM subjects. This effect may be particularly strong for populations that have historically struggled in STEM classes and that are historically underrepresented in STEM programs in higher education and STEM professions. However, studies on identity in the context of integrated STEM education are few, and most of them are qualitative in nature. In addition, outcomes focused on interest and identity are more commonly measured in after- and out-of-school settings than in the context of formal classrooms.

IMPLICATIONS OF RESEARCH FOR THE DESIGN OF INTEGRATED STEM EDUCATION

In addition to reviewing research related to outcomes, the committee examined research from cognitive psychology, the learning sciences, and educational psychology—as well as from studies focused specifically on integrated STEM education—for clues about factors that may help explain the potential benefits and challenges posed by integration.

From the perspective of what is currently known about cognition and learning, integration may be effective because basic qualities of cognition favor connected concepts over unconnected concepts so they are better organized for future retrieval and meaning making. It is these connected knowledge structures that can support learners' ability to transfer understanding and competencies to new or unfamiliar situations. In addition, being able to represent the same concept within and across disciplines in multiple ways—for example, visually, in physical form, and in writing—can facilitate learning, research shows. But integration can also impede learning because it can place excessive demands on resource-limited cognitive processes, such as attention and working memory.

Though fundamental to all learning experiences, social and cultural experiences such as those which require students to work with each other and actively engage in discussion, joint decision making, and collaborative problem solving may be particularly important in integrated learning. Some social processes can support learning through deliberate efforts to convey knowledge and strategies to children. Techniques such as scaffolding and peer collaboration can help students be successful with challenging tasks and move beyond their current state of knowledge.

One hallmark of integrated approaches, though not unique to them, is the use of real-world situations or problems. Although these contexts can bring STEM fields alive for students and have the potential to deepen their learning, they may also pose challenges to students. For instance, there is evidence that use of detailed concrete situations that include rich perceptual information can prevent students from identifying the abstract structural characteristics that are needed to transfer their experiences to other settings.

Taken together, the findings from research have implications for the design of integrated STEM education initiatives. Three key implications are:

1. Integration should be made explicit. Observations in a number of STEM settings show that integration across representations and materials, as well as over the arc of multi-day units, is not spontaneously made by students and therefore cannot be assumed to take place. This highlights the importance of designing integrated experiences that provide intentional and explicit support for students to build knowledge and skill both within the disciplines and across disciplines. In many integrated STEM experiences, such supports are missing or only implicitly embedded within the classroom activities or the CAD software, measurement instruments, and computational tools used in the classroom.
2. Students' knowledge in individual disciplines must be supported. Connecting ideas across disciplines is challenging when students have little or no understanding of the relevant ideas in the individual disciplines. Also, students do not always or naturally use their disciplinary knowledge in integrated contexts. Students will thus need support to elicit the relevant scientific or mathematical ideas in an engineering or technological design context, to connect those ideas productively, and to reorganize their own ideas in ways that come to reflect normative, scientific ideas and practices.
3. More integration is not necessarily better. The potential benefits and challenges of making connections across the STEM subjects suggest the importance of a measured, strategic approach to implementing integrated STEM education that accounts for the potential trade-offs in cognition and learning.

CONTEXT FOR IMPLEMENTING INTEGRATED
STEM EDUCATION EXPERIENCES

Three contextual factors are likely to present both opportunities and challenges to the implementation of integrated STEM education at the K–12
level: standards, assessments, and educator supports.

The recently published CCSSM and the NGSS have the potential to focus
educators on helping students make connections across the disciplines. The
committee recognizes that not all states will adopt the CCSSM or the NGSS.
However, the underlying principles that inform both sets of standards are
likely to influence approaches to mathematics and science education, even in
those states that do not formally adopt the new standards. These underlying
principles include active engagement of students in authentic tasks, support
for development of conceptual knowledge and reasoning, and application of
knowledge in real-world contexts.

One challenge of taking advantage of the opportunities for integration
presented by the CCSSM and NGSS is attending to developing disciplinary
knowledge while also supporting students in making connections across
disciplines. This concern is highlighted by research showing that curricula
integrating mathematics or science with other STEM subjects are less likely
to produce positive learning outcomes in mathematics than they are in science, although effect sizes can vary greatly depending on how science and
mathematics are offered (sequentially, in parallel, together and separately,
or together either with one subject as the dominant theme of the lesson
or with both subjects completely integrated—see Chapter 3 for additional
details). A second challenge is presented by the partial overlap in some of
the practices identified in the CCSSM and NGSS, where the same terms
have different meanings for experts in different fields. For example, argumentation in mathematics differs from argumentation in science. In order
for students to engage in argumentation in both disciplines, they will need
to understand what makes scientific arguments different from mathematical arguments.

Assessments—from formative assessment at the classroom level to
large-scale state assessment for accountability—have the potential to limit
the extent to which integrated STEM can be incorporated into K–12 education. Existing assessments tend to focus on knowledge in a single discipline.
Furthermore, they typically focus on content knowledge alone and give little
attention to the practices in the disciplines and applications of knowledge.
In terms of innovative approaches, large-scale assessments pose the biggest

challenges, though some innovative examples do exist, such as the National Assessment of Educational Progress (NAEP) probe assessment of technology and engineering literacy being fielded in a sample of US eighth graders in 2014. Other potential models of assessments that might be adapted to address STEM integration include the recently restructured advanced placement (AP) biology exam from the College Board and the computer-based tasks on the 2009 NAEP Interactive Computer and Hands-On Tasks Science Assessment. More generally, digital and networking technologies have the potential to expand the range of outcomes (e.g., progressions of integrated STEM learning) that can be measured.

The expertise of educators working in classrooms and in after-/out-of-school settings is a key factor—some would say *the* key factor—in determining whether integrated STEM education can be done in ways that produce positive outcomes for students. One limiting factor to teacher effectiveness and self-efficacy is teachers' content knowledge in the subjects being taught. For example, most K–12 science and mathematics teachers have taken fewer courses in the subject area(s) in which they were prepared than are recommended by their respective teacher professional associations, and many have taken few courses in other areas of STEM. The small amount of available data for K–12 technology teachers, many of whom are providing engineering instruction, suggests their preparation in mathematics and science is quite limited. Furthermore, surveys find that teachers of K–12 mathematics and science lack confidence in their ability to teach engineering.

Apart from subject-specific content knowledge, the ability and confidence to teach across subjects will be critical for educators called upon to deliver integrated K–12 STEM education. Educators will need to know how to provide instructional supports that help students recognize connections between disciplines, and they will need to support students' developing proficiency in individual subjects in ways that complement students' learning through integrated activities. At the present time, very few teacher education programs around the country are making efforts to prepare prospective teachers with appropriate content knowledge in more than one STEM subject. A larger number of programs provides in-service professional development related to integrated STEM education; most of these efforts are connected to existing curriculum projects.

Although perhaps obvious, it is worth noting that many of the changes likely to be needed to successfully implement integrated STEM education will require additional financial resources. Money, as well as time and planning, will be required to help educators acquire content and pedagogical content knowledge in disciplinary areas beyond their previous education or experience. And funds will be needed to design, pilot test, and implement any large-scale assessment.

RECOMMENDATIONS

The committee developed 10 recommendations: two directed at multiple stakeholders in K–12 integrated STEM education; four directed at those involved in designing integrated STEM education initiatives; one intended for those charged with developing assessments; and three that target researchers. In the full report, the recommendations appear in Chapter 6 in an order different from that presented here. For clarity, the number of the recommendation as it appears in the full report is indicated.

Recommendations for Multiple Stakeholders

Researchers, program designers, and practitioners focused on integrated STEM education, and the professional organizations that represent them, need to develop a common language to describe their work. This report can serve as a starting point. (Recommendation 2)

To allow for continuous and meaningful improvement, designers of integrated STEM education initiatives, those charged with implementing such efforts, and organizations that fund the interventions should explicitly ground their efforts in an iterative model of educational improvement. (Recommendation 10)

Recommendations for Designers of Integrated STEM Experiences

Designers of integrated STEM education initiatives need to be explicit about the goals they aim to achieve and design the integrated STEM experience purposefully to achieve these goals. They also need to better articulate their hypotheses about why and how a particular integrated STEM experience will lead to particular outcomes and how those outcomes should be measured. (Recommendation 5)

Designers of integrated STEM education initiatives need to build in opportunities that make STEM connections explicit to students and educators (e.g., through appropriate scaffolding and sufficient opportunities to engage in activities that address connected ideas). (Recommendation 6)

Designers of integrated STEM experiences need to attend to the learning goals and learning progressions in the individual STEM subjects so as not to inadvertently undermine student learning in those subjects. (Recommendation 7)

Programs that prepare people to deliver integrated STEM instruction need to provide experiences that help these educators identify and make explicit to their students connections among the disciplines. These educators will also need opportunities and training to work collaboratively with their colleagues, and in some cases administrators or curriculum coordinators will need to play a role in creating these opportunities. Finally, some forms of professional development may need to be designed as partnerships among between educators, STEM professionals, and researchers. (Recommendation 8)

Recommendation for Assessment Developers

Organizations with expertise in assessment research and development should create assessments appropriate to measuring the various learning and affective outcomes of integrated STEM education. This work should involve not only the modification of existing tools and techniques but also exploration of novel approaches. Federal agencies with a major role in supporting STEM education in the United States, such as the Department of Education and the National Science Foundation, should consider supporting these efforts. (Recommendation 9)

Recommendations for Researchers

In future studies of integrated STEM education, researchers need to document the curriculum, program, or other intervention in greater detail, with particular attention to the nature of the integration and how it was supported. When reporting on outcomes, researchers should be explicit about the nature of the integration, the types of scaffolds and instructional designs used, and the type of evidence collected to demonstrate whether the goals of the intervention were achieved. Specific learning mechanisms should be articulated and supporting evidence provided for them. (Recommendation 1)

Study outcomes should be identified from the outset based on clearly articulated hypotheses about the mechanisms by which integrated STEM education supports learning, thinking, interest, identity, and persistence. Measures should be selected or developed based on these outcomes. (Recommendation 3)

Research on integrated STEM education that is focused on interest and identity should include more longitudinal studies, use multiple methods, including design experiments, and address diversity and equity. (Recommendation 4)

RESEARCH AGENDA

To help guide future research, the committee posed questions aligned to the descriptive framework that, if addressed, have the potential to provide useful data for advancing the quality and effectiveness of integrated K–12 STEM education in the United States. The questions fall under three broad categories referenced earlier: outcomes of integrated STEM education, the nature of integrated STEM education, and design and implementation of integrated STEM education. Within each category, specific research questions are identified. For example, "What instructional approaches or contexts are most likely to lead to student outcomes related to making connections between and among the STEM disciplines?" And, "How should integrated STEM experiences be designed to account for educators' and students' varying levels of experience with integrated learning and STEM content?" Taken together, the questions comprise a research agenda for integrated STEM education.

FINAL THOUGHTS

There is much more that can and should be learned about the outcomes, nature, and design and implementation of integrated STEM education. This should not discourage those designing, implementing, or studying integrated STEM education programs. On the contrary, our findings, recommendations, and research agenda strongly suggest the *potential* of some forms of integrated STEM education to make a positive difference in learning, interest, and other valued outcomes.

The level of evidence gathered by the committee is not sufficient to suggest that integrated STEM education could or should replace high-quality education focused on individual STEM subjects. Indeed, integrated STEM education requires that students hone their expertise in the very disciplines that are being connected. However, parts of the STEM education community are already moving toward integration. This suggests that the energy, creativity, and resources of researchers, practitioners, and concerned funders should be directed at generating more thoughtful, high-quality, and evidence-based work exploring the benefits and limitations of integrated STEM education. Given the inherent complexities, it will not be a surprise to find that designing and documenting effective initiatives will be time consuming and expensive. Despite these challenges, the possibility of adding new tools to the STEM education toolbox is exciting and should be coupled with rigorous research and assessment of implementation efforts.

1

Introduction

Education in science, technology, engineering, and mathematics has received growing attention over the past decade, with calls both for greater emphasis on these fields and for improvements in curricula and instruction within and across them. In the policy arena and increasingly among educators, these subjects together are referred to as STEM (Box 1-1).

Multiple reports issued by influential education, policy, and business groups have argued the case for expanding and improving STEM education (e.g., AAAS 1990, 1993; Carnegie Corporation 2009; Council on Competitiveness 2005; NCMSTC 2000; NGA 2007; NRC 1996, 2007a, 2012a; NSB 2007; PCAST 2012). Among other things, the case rests on the idea that a STEM education can lead to productive employment and is critical to the nation's innovation capacity. And many employers and public officials have come to believe that all people, particularly young people, needs to have some degree of scientific and technological literacy in order to lead productive lives as citizens, whether or not they ever work in a STEM-related field. In today's science- and technology-rich society, such literacy is important to being a smart consumer and thoughtful participant in democratic decision making and to making sense of the world more generally. Thus STEM education serves to prepare a scientific and technical workforce, where integration is becoming increasingly common in cutting-edge research and development (Box 1-2), as well as a scientifically and technologically literate and more informed society.

BOX 1-1
The Four STEM Disciplines

Science is the study of the natural world, including the laws of nature associated with physics, chemistry, and biology and the treatment or application of facts, principles, concepts, or conventions associated with these disciplines. Science is both a body of knowledge that has been accumulated over time and a process—scientific inquiry—that generates new knowledge. Knowledge from science informs the engineering design process.

Technology, while not a discipline in the strictest sense, comprises the entire system of people and organizations, knowledge, processes, and devices that go into creating and operating technological artifacts, as well as the artifacts themselves. Throughout history, humans have created technology to satisfy their wants and needs. Much of modern technology is a product of science and engineering, and technological tools are used in both fields.

Engineering is both a body of knowledge—about the design and creation of human-made products—and a process for solving problems. This process is design under constraint. One constraint in engineering design is the laws of nature, or science. Other constraints include time, money, available materials, ergonomics, environmental regulations, manufacturability, and reparability. Engineering utilizes concepts in science and mathematics as well as technological tools.

Mathematics is the study of patterns and relationships among quantities, numbers, and space. Unlike in science, where empirical evidence is sought to warrant or overthrow claims, claims in mathematics are warranted through logical arguments based on foundational assumptions. The logical arguments themselves are part of mathematics along with the claims. As in science, knowledge in mathematics continues to grow, but unlike in science, knowledge in mathematics is not overturned, unless the foundational assumptions are transformed. Specific conceptual categories of K–12 mathematics include numbers and arithmetic, algebra, functions, geometry, and statistics and probability. Mathematics is used in science, engineering, and technology.

SOURCE: Adapted from NRC (2009).

BOX 1-2
The New Biology

... (t)he essence of the New Biology is integration—re-integration of the many subdisciplines of biology, and the integration into biology of physicists, chemists, computer scientists, engineers, and mathematicians to create a research community with the capacity to tackle a broad range of scientific and societal problems.

SOURCE: NRC (2009, p. vii).

Efforts to improve science and mathematics education in grades K–12 are not new. Since the 1960s these efforts have included curriculum development projects, professional development networks, and the creation of national standards documents (e.g., AAAS 1993; NCTM 1989; NRC 1996). The release of the *Common Core State Standards for Mathematics* (NGACPB 2010) and the *Next Generation Science Standards* (NGSS; Achieve 2013), the latter modeled on *A Framework for K–12 Science Education: Practices, Crosscutting Concepts, and Core Ideas* (NRC 2012a), have further focused the nation's attention on teaching and learning of these subjects. In engineering and technology the emphasis has been on expanding attention to these disciplines at the pre-college level, including through development of educational standards (e.g., ITEEA 2000), and making the case that exposing students to the E and T of STEM has the potential to improve learning of science and mathematics (NAE and NRC, 2009).

Yet, despite the increased attention to STEM in policy and funding arenas, there remains some confusion about STEM, the individual subjects, the combination of the subjects, and even what constitutes STEM.[1] In particular, recent use of the term has raised interest in whether there is something to be gained from considering the disciplines together, as somehow connected or integrated, rather than continuing to look at each separately in both teaching and learning. This report examines current initiatives in integrated STEM education and the evidence of their impacts.

---

[1] It is worth noting that while the STEM acronym is gaining currency in policy and education circles, many Americans do not associate the term with education at all but with very different ideas, such as stem cell research and a part of a plant (Keefe 2009).

STEM IN THE K–12 CURRICULUM

Efforts to make connections among the STEM subjects are complicated by the history of the K–12 curriculum and the "place" of each of the disciplines within it. The roots of today's curriculum date back to the work of the Harvard Committee of Ten (NEA 1894), which stressed learning in discrete subject areas. This focus on individual disciplines is important, because there is great complexity and much to be understood about how students acquire knowledge and skills in each area. Each discipline comprises a knowledge base, specialized practices, and particular habits of mind. It seems appropriate and necessary, then, that efforts to understand and improve discipline-focused STEM education continue.[2] At the same time, the historical focus on the individual disciplines, which has influenced decades of curriculum development and teacher education, presents practical challenges to making cross-disciplinary connections in K–12 STEM education.

Mathematics Education

Mathematics instruction—commonly addressing arithmetic, geometry, algebra, trigonometry, and calculus—has been a regular part of K–12 education in the United States since the early 1900s (Stanic and Kilpatrick 1992). During the elementary years the same teacher usually teaches all of the core subjects, including mathematics. Since the 2001 No Child Left Behind (NCLB) Act required regular testing in mathematics, the subject has received greater attention in elementary school, though it still is not typically given as much time in the school day as reading and language arts. For example, on the 2011 National Assessment of Educational Progress, 4th-grade teachers reported the amount of instructional time in each subject. In reading, 49 percent of teachers reported providing more than 10 hours per week of language arts instruction, whereas only 29 percent of teachers reported spending more than 7 hours per week on mathematics instruction—most (59 percent) reported spending 5 to 6.9 hours per week (Ginsberg and Chudowsky 2012)

Starting in middle school or junior high and continuing into high school, mathematics is taught as separate classes with specialized teachers. Most states require proficiency in algebra in order to graduate from high school, and students often follow different mathematics sequences that vary in content and level or rigor.

---

[2] Such efforts at the undergraduate level are synthesized in NRC 2012b.

As of 2008, the 43 states with graduation requirements in mathematics required at least two years of courses in that subject (with one exception, Illinois, which required only one year) (NSF 2012).

Science Education

Science education—commonly addressing biology, chemistry, physics, and Earth and space sciences—although not as prevalent in US schools as mathematics education, also has been a regular part of most K–12 students' school experiences. However, science has not typically received much attention in elementary school, particularly in grades K–2. It is usually taught by the same teacher who teaches reading, mathematics, and social studies. As with mathematics, specialized science classes begin in middle/junior high school.

The 44 states with science graduation requirements required two or more years of courses in that subject (NSF 2012). Testing in science under NCLB was mandated later (2007) than for mathematics and reading (2003) and at a much lower frequency. Unlike the testing for mathematics and reading, science was never part of the "adequate yearly progress" requirement that holds schools accountable for students' progress from year to year. Over the past decade, there has been a trend in elementary schools toward spending less time on science and more time on reading and mathematics, presumably due at least in part to the NCLB legislation (Blank 2012).

Technology Education

Education related to technology—the T in STEM—is interpreted and addressed in a variety of ways. Prior to the mid-1980s the school subject known as technology education was called industrial arts and, before that, manual arts. Some current versions of technology education are similar to and often confused with vocational education, which has a long and separate history in the United States as a trade or job skills program. In the past decade, however, much of vocational education has been adopting a more academic program of study, including material related to the STEM subjects, under the label of career and technical education, or CTE.

Moreover, technology teachers today are a varied group. Some oversee traditional laboratories where students build artifacts from wood, metal, plastic, and other materials. Others present a broader perspective on technology and its interaction with society, viewing technology as key to understanding topics such as manufacturing, construction, transportation, and telecommunication. Over the past decade, prompted in part by publication of the *Standards for Technological Literacy* (ITEEA 2000) and the development of national programs such as Project Lead the Way,[3] some technology teachers have begun to teach engineering.

Another interpretation of the T in STEM is what many refer to as educational, or instructional, technology. Over the years, such technologies have included filmstrips, movies, television, videos, and learning aids such as calculators and electronic white boards. Arguably, the most influential educational technologies to date are the personal computer and the Internet, including online resources and educational software. Continual improvements in processing speeds and data storage, lower price points, the advent of the fast, wireless Internet, and cloud computing have combined to make PCs (as well as laptops, tablet computers, and smartphones) a central tool for learning both in and out of the classroom.

Computers, software, sensors, and other data collection instruments are also a major component of yet a third interpretation of technology relevant to STEM education: the tools used by practitioners of science, mathematics, and engineering. These tools include everything from scales used to accurately measure the volume or mass of substances, to microscopes and telescopes used to study very small and very far objects, to supercomputers used to model complex phenomena such as weather, and particle accelerators that reveal the tiniest building blocks of matter.

Engineering Education

The newest and least developed component of the STEM quartet at the K–12 level is engineering. Its footprint in elementary and secondary schools is much smaller than those of mathematics, science, and technology. Most of the growth in efforts to teach engineering to children has occurred over the past 15 years, as a number of engineering-focused curricula have been designed and implemented in elementary and secondary schools across the nation (see NAE and NRC 2009 for more information about these efforts). And a small but growing number of initiatives is providing professional development to teachers to enable them to engage students in engineering activities.

---

[3] More information about this initiative is available at www.pltw.org/.

There is no formal agreement on what constitutes engineering knowledge and skills at the K–12 level, but there is growing recognition of the importance of the engineering design process and of concepts such as constraints, criteria, optimization, and trade-offs. As of 2010, nine states had incorporated engineering in their standards for science education (NAE 2010). The NGSS (Achieve 2013) includes engineering concepts and practices alongside those of science. Twenty-six states participated in the development of the standards, and many of these are expected to adopt them, potentially paving the way for greater inclusion of engineering education at the K–12 level.

CONNECTIONS IN STEM EDUCATION

While most new programs and specialized schools continue to address one or more of the STEM subjects separately, there have been some attempts to highlight connections within, between, and among[4] the STEM subjects as well. Several reasons are often cited for this emphasis.

Although their efforts were focused on science rather than STEM, previous NRC committees have offered visions of how learning about science can incorporate habits of mind and practices along with the acquisition of content knowledge that can be viewed as integrative and contributing to building of skills that would be useful in the workplace. For example, the authoring committee for *Taking Science to School: Learning and Teaching Science in Grades K–8* (NRC 2007b) recommended that science teaching and curriculum should include the following four strands of scientific proficiency as a framework for learning within those disciplines:

- Know, use, and interpret scientific explanations of the natural world.
- Generate and evaluate scientific evidence and explanations.
- Understand the nature and development of scientific knowledge.
- Participate productively in scientific practices and discourse.

These strands are not to be viewed as components that need to be taught independently. Rather, the committee recommended that science learning be developed in ways in which all of the strands are inextricably intertwined.

---

[4] The committee uses "between" and "among" in recognition that some integrated STEM education initiatives involve connections between only two of the STEM disciplines, while others involve connections among three or more.

The committee that authored *Learning Science in Informal Environments: People, Places, and Pursuits* (NRC 2009b) embraced these strands and added two additional ones:

- Experience excitement, interest, and motivation to learn about phenomena in the natural and physical world.
- Think about themselves as science learners and develop an identity as someone who knows about, uses, and sometimes contributes to science.

Advocates of more integrated approaches to teaching and learning, both within and across disciplines, note that the professional practices that inspired the focus on individual disciplines have been transformed in many workplace and research settings to emphasize multidisciplinary enterprises, such as biomedical engineering. More generally, many real-world contexts and problems typically involve more than one of the disciplines. For example, designing alternative energy systems that run on solar or wind energy, understanding how to maintain a clean water supply, or maintaining fragile ecosystems will require knowledge and practices from across the STEM disciplines.

Moreover, professional scientists and engineers in the vast, interconnected enterprise of companies, academic institutions, and government laboratories that conduct research and develop new products and services almost always work in ways that integrate the disciplines of STEM. In fact in some research areas the necessity of more interdisciplinary approaches is increasing. In the life sciences, for example, there is recognition that some of the most important and interesting questions in modern biology will require closer interaction not only within the subdisciplines in biology but also among professionals in biology, chemistry, physics, computer science, mathematics, and engineering (NRC 2009a). Similar interactions among earth, behavioral, and social sciences also will become increasingly essential to addressing critical issues facing humanity and the planet.

More generally, scientists use technological tools to conduct experiments and mathematics and statistics to interpret the data produced by those experiments; engineers draw on scientific knowledge and mathematical reasoning to develop and model potential design inventions and solutions; technologists who build and maintain the products and systems designed by engineers must understand the scientific and mathematical principles governing their operation. And these professionals interact with one another in increasingly diverse and multidisciplinary teams. Connections among the

STEM disciplines extend beyond the workplace. In their day-to-day affairs, citizens encounter situations that require them to make decisions using a mix of STEM-related knowledge and skills—whether choosing appropriate medical care, interpreting statistical data in the latest political poll, or buying energy-saving appliances. Indeed, the arguments for general scientific and technological literacy, and for numeracy, have been well articulated (e.g., AAAS 1991; NAE and NRC 2002; NRC 1989). Advocates of more integrated approaches to K–12 STEM education claim it has advantages for learning and motivation. They contend that teaching STEM in the context of real-world issues and challenges[5]—and hence, in an integrated fashion—can make the subjects more relevant to students and teachers, thereby enhancing motivation for learning and improving student achievement and persistence. These effects, in turn, may enhance workplace and college readiness skills and increase the number of students who consider a career in a STEM-related field. These issues are discussed in greater detail in Chapter 3.

Efforts to integrate across the STEM disciplines are not entirely new but until relatively recently focused largely on connecting just science and mathematics; for example, the School Science and Mathematics Association (www.ssma.org) has been a locus for discussions of such integration since its founding in 1901. As recently as 20 years ago, at the launch of the standards-based education reform movement, there was recognition of the value of integration in STEM beyond just mathematics and science. *Benchmarks for Science Literacy*, for example, defined science as "basic and applied natural and social science, basic and applied mathematics, and engineering and technology, and the interconnections—which is to say the scientific enterprise as a whole" (AAAS 1993, p. 321). Both *Benchmarks* and the *National Science Education Standards* (NRC 1996) called for student learning related to "technology and society" and "technological design"—in *science* classes. The *Standards for Technological Literacy* (ITEEA 2000) devoted significant sections to spelling out learning goals related to engineering design and stressed the need for students to understand technology's connections to science, engineering, and mathematics.

More recently, the NGSS calls for deeper connections among mathematics, science, and engineering, and it encourages making connections between the subdisciplines of science, such as how energy is understood in biology

---

[5] By real world, we mean that a student will perceive the challenge posed as worthy of solution, not necessarily that the challenge copies exactly the complexities or subtleties of what takes place in science or engineering research or in commercial or academic technology development enterprises.

and physics. As noted, the standards explicitly include practices and core ideas from engineering that should be taught in science classrooms. The *Common Core State Standards* (NGACPB 2010) in mathematics also suggest opportunities for making connections among the STEM subjects. For instance, the practice labeled "model with mathematics" calls for students to "apply the mathematics they know to solve problems arising in everyday life, society, and the workplace," which will necessarily involve ideas and practices from science, engineering, or technology.

Despite the arguments for making connections across the STEM disciplines and the increased number of efforts to design learning experiences that will foster such connections, there is little research on how best to do so or on whether more explicit connections or integration across the disciplines significantly improves student learning, retention, achievement, or other valued outcomes. Recognizing the need for a more robust evidence base, the National Academy of Engineering and the Board on Science Education of the National Research Council convened a committee to examine current efforts to connect the STEM disciplines in K–12 education through integrated approaches and to develop a research agenda that will provide the data needed to inform such efforts.

COMMITTEE CHARGE

The Committee on Integrated STEM Education was charged with developing a research agenda for determining the approaches and conditions most likely to lead to positive outcomes of integrated STEM education at the K–12 level.[6] The specific objectives of the project were as follows:

- Identify and characterize existing approaches to integrated STEM education, in both formal and after-school and informal[7] settings.
- Review the evidence for the impact of integrated approaches on various parameters of interest, such as increasing student awareness, interest, motivation, and achievement in STEM subjects; improving college readiness skills; and boosting the number and quality of students who may consider a career in a STEM-related field.

---

[6] The committee limited its data gathering and analysis to efforts taking place in the United States.

[7] The committee considered informal settings to include both those in after-school and out-of-school environments.

- Determine a set of priority research questions to advance understanding of the impacts of integrated STEM education.
- Propose methodological approaches for addressing these questions.
- Identify potential parties who could carry out the research.

DETERMINING THE SCOPE OF THE CHARGE

Developing a precise definition of integrated STEM education proved to be a challenge for the committee because of the multiple ways such integration can occur. It may include different combinations of the STEM disciplines, emphasize one discipline more than another, be presented in a formal or informal setting, and involve a range of pedagogical strategies. For example, one model suggests that "integrative" STEM education must include technological or engineering design as a basis for creating connections to concepts and practices from mathematics or science (or both) (Sanders 2009).

In educational practice and in research, the term *integrated* is used loosely and is typically not carefully distinguished from related terms such as *connected, unified, interdisciplinary, multidisciplinary, cross-disciplinary,* or *transdisciplinary*. Defining integrated STEM education is further complicated by the fact that connections can be reflected at more than one level at the same time: in the student's thinking or behavior, in the teacher's instruction, in the curriculum, between and among teachers themselves, or in larger units of the education system, such as the organization of an entire school. The multidimensional nature of integrated STEM education led to one of the major tasks for the committee, "to identify and characterize existing approaches to integrated STEM." Chapter 2 of this report takes up this element of the charge.

While the committee was unable to achieve consensus on a concise and useful definition of integrated STEM education, it still needed to determine which programs, studies, and evaluations to consider under the umbrella of integrated STEM education. In doing so the committee members acknowledged that they would likely find relevant programs or interventions not explicitly labeled "integrated" that would nevertheless provide important insights about ways to support students in making connections across the STEM disciplines. In the end, the committee chose to use a broad, inclusive lens to guide its examination of integrated STEM education. Details about the literature search and the process of identifying programs are provided in the next section.

The committee discussed the possibility that the report's lack of a strict definition might result in schools and programs engaged in STEM education claiming integration without actually doing it. This is a real risk. But in the committee's view, at this early stage of the field's development, it is less problematic than proposing a definition that artificially—or unwisely—constricts the type of experimentation and creativity that will be needed in research and practice to advance our understanding of integrated STEM education.

Over the course of the study, the committee came to recognize that it was important to consider integration in terms of both the design of the learning experiences and the anticipated student outcomes. In many cases, an experience may have been labeled "integrated" because the activities for students involved ideas and practices from more than one discipline, but learning outcomes (or other outcomes) were measured in only one discipline. The committee also found examples where curriculum or program designers may have stated their intention to create an integrated experience but the learner did not experience or recognize such. We discuss the implications of both of these situations in Chapters 3 and 4.

The committee also noted a tendency in the literature on integrated STEM education to conflate particular pedagogies with integration. For example, authors and program developers seemed to assume that adopting a problem- or project-based approach automatically meant disciplinary integration. It was not clear to the committee that this was necessarily the case. For this reason, the members tried to specify and carefully describe both the pedagogical approach and the kind of integration that various interventions and programs intended.

While the focus of this report is integrated STEM education, the committee in no way wishes to suggest that integrated STEM education should supplant learning in the individual STEM disciplines, which is appropriate in many situations. Part of the challenge of integrated STEM education—and of this report—is in determining the appropriate timing, contexts, and purposes where integrated approaches provide value beyond what students might learn by studying the disciplines individually. And while the committee was aware of a number of efforts to integrate one or more STEM subjects with others such as English language arts, art, and history, with few exceptions we restricted our analysis to integration involving only the STEM subjects.

Finally, this report raises many more questions than it answers regarding integrated STEM education, as is appropriate for a topic that has received relatively little systematic attention in the research literature. As a result, the report does not recommend specific approaches or implementation strategies for integrated STEM education.

THE STUDY PROCESS

To carry out the charge, the committee met five times over an 18-month period, held three information-gathering sessions, and commissioned topical papers relevant to its work.

The information-gathering sessions brought in speakers from around the country to present and discuss work relevant to integrated STEM education. In addition to discussions of specific programs, curricula, and school-based efforts, presenters addressed topics such as diversity in integrated STEM education, the role of technology in STEM education, the potential for integration in STEM standards, and challenges to implementing integrated STEM education.

In developing this report, the committee worked with outside consultant David Heil and Associates (DHA), who oversaw reviews of the research literature related to integrated STEM education in both formal and after- and out-of-school settings (e.g., robotics competitions, science and technology centers); DHA also oversaw a review of the cognitive sciences literature related to integrated STEM education. The literature review began with a search using the major multidisciplinary search engines such as Scopus, Web of Science, and INSPEC and was designed to capture a broad range of studies. The search used combinations of the following terms: integrated curriculum; integrated education; integrative; cross-disciplinary; inter-disciplinary; multidisciplinary; project-based; K–12 education; unified studies curriculum; STEM; STEM education; integrated STEM education; science, mathematics, technology, and engineering education; inquiry-based instruction and learning; constructivism; cognitive development; cognition; learning; achievement; informal education; non-formal education; mentor; out-of-school; after school; enrichment; and extracurricular.

Overall, multiple searches in the formal education, informal education, and cognitive areas uncovered over 500 reference citations. The abstracts of these articles were reviewed to glean more information about content and relevance. Papers were initially included if the program described or studied integrated at least two STEM subjects. Four other criteria were also considered:

- Does the integration include engineering as one of the integrated subjects?
- Does the article provide empirical evidence regarding the impact of the program or a review of research on integrated curriculum?
- Do the authors present information or insights that are likely to contribute to addressing the committee's charge?
- Is the focus of the article on K–12 education and/or informal education programs?

Articles were more likely to be considered if they met more of the criteria. This initial search of the literature was supplemented by searches using key authors suggested by the committee or identified in articles as search terms.

The literature review was complemented by commissioned papers on social cognition, embodied cognition, the development of interest and identity, and assessment. The committee considered the literature review and the commissioned papers together in developing the report.

Also, with guidance from the committee, DHA identified a large sample of programs, projects, schools, and other initiatives that claimed or appeared to be engaged in integrated STEM education. Of 213 possible programs or initiatives, 55 were dropped because they did not appear to be integrated, no current information was available, or they did not have any evidence of impact. The remaining 158 programs were formal education programs (98), informal education programs (46), and programs that combined formal and informal elements in some way (14). From this group and taking account of time and budget constraints, DHA selected 28 (14 formal and 14 informal) to be reviewed in greater detail (Appendix; excerpts from some of these reviews appear throughout the report). The selection was based on expert judgment, the information available for each program, the responsiveness of program developers or practitioners to inquiries, evidence of integration, and some evidence of program impacts. In addition, programs were selected to represent different types and scales of integration. Formal education programs were identified as activities, modules, full curriculum, school-wide programs, or teacher preparation/professional development. Informal program categories included curriculum, professional development, after-school, camps, community events, competitions, exhibit/on-site drop-in programs, mentoring/internships, and media (e.g., television, websites).

Finally, the committee's understanding of integrated STEM education and how to make this report useful to readers was informed by interviews

DHA conducted with some 30 stakeholders in education, policymaking, and industry.

THE REPORT

Chapter 2 of this report presents a descriptive framework for integrated STEM education. The framework can be used to help design and study such integrated approaches. Chapter 3 focuses on evidence most closely related to integrated STEM education, considering outcomes related to learning, achievement, interest, and identity. Chapter 4 explores a broader range of literatures and identifies potential implications for the design of integrated STEM learning experiences. Both chapters draw on the DHA literature review and commissioned papers as well as the committee's expertise. Chapter 5 discusses the context for integrated STEM education, considering standards, assessment, and supports for teachers. Chapter 6 summarizes key findings based on the evidence discussed in the previous chapters and presents recommendations and a research agenda developed by the committee.

APPENDIX

List of Reviewed Programs[8]

Formal Programs

Active Physics (http://its-about-time.com/physics/ap.html)
A World in Motion® (www.awim.org)
Biological Sciences Curriculum Study (www.bscs.org)
Engineering by Design—EbD-TEEMS™ (www.engineeringbydesign.org)
Engineering is Elementary (www.eie.org/)
Engineering the Future (www.mos.org/etf/)
Everyday STEM (www.shop.pitsco.com/store/item.aspx?art=4725)
Engaging Youth through Engineering (www.maef.net)
Harrisonburg Public Schools (www.i-stem-harrisonburg.com/)
I-STEM Summer Institute (www.sde.idaho.gov/site/istem)
Integrated Mathematics, Science, and Technology (http://cemast.
    illinoisstate.edu/educators/stem/index.shtml)

---

[8] Accessed November 15, 2013.

Manor New Tech High (http://mnths.manorisd.net)
The National Center for STEM Elementary Education (www.stem.stkate.
    edu/stk/center.php)
WISEngineering (www.wisengineering.org)

Informal Programs

Build IT (http://buildit.sri.com/index.html)
Camp Invention (www.invent.org)
CSTEM Challenge (www.cstem.org)
Design It! (http://npass2.edc.org/resources/design-it)
Design Squad Nation (www.pbskids.org/designsquad/)
DREAM—Achievement Through Mentorship (http://.dream.rice.edu)
Family Engineering[9] (www.familyengineering.org)
Jr. FIRST LEGO League, FIRST LEGO League, FIRST Tech Challenge,
    FIRST Robotics Competition (www.usfirst.org)
MathAlive! (www.mathalive.com)
National Partnerships for Afterschool Science (NPASS) and NPASS2
    (http://.npass2.edc.org)
Techbridge (www.techbridgegirls.org)
TechXcite (www.techxcite.org)
Tinkerer's Workshop[10]
Waterbotics[11] (www.waterbotics.org)

REFERENCES

AAAS (American Association for the Advancement of Science). 1990. Science for All
    Americans. New York: Oxford University Press.
AAAS. 1993. Benchmarks for Science Literacy. New York: Oxford University Press.
Achieve, Inc. 2013. Next Generation Science Standards. Available at www.nextgenscience.
    org/next-generation-science-standards (retrieved July 17, 2013).

---

[9] David Heil and Associates, the contractor that oversaw the literature reviews and conducted the programs reviews for this project, helped develop and conducted a formative
evaluation of the Family Engineering program.

[10] This long-running exhibit at the Austin Children's Museum (now, The Thinkery),
which emphasized the processes of tinkering and engineering design, no longer exists.

[11] Waterbotics was developed by Stevens Institute of Technology's Center for Innovation
in Engineering and Science Education, where committee member Beth McGrath was director at the time the reviews were conducted.

Blank, R. 2012. What is the impact of decline in science instructional time in elementary school? Time for elementary instruction has declined, and less time for science is correlated with lower scores on NAEP. Paper prepared for the Noyce Foundation. Available at www.csss-science.org/downloads/NAEPElemScienceData.pdf (retrieved July 17, 2013).

Carnegie Corporation of New York. 2009. The Opportunity Equation: Transforming Mathematics and Science Education for Citizenship and the Global Economy. Available at http://opportunityequation.org/uploads/files/oe_report.pdf (retrieved August 14, 2013).

Council on Competitiveness. 2005. Innovate America. Available at www.compete.org/images/uploads/File/PDF%20Files/NII_Innovate_America.pdf (retrieved August 14, 2013).

Ginsberg, A., and N. Chudowsky. 2012. Time for Learning: An Exploratory Analysis of NAEP Data. Prepared for the National Assessment Governing Board. Available at www.nagb.org/content/nagb/assets/documents/what-we-do/quarterly-board-meeting-materials/2012-11/time-for-learning-naep-data-analysis.pdf (retrieved November 14, 2013).

ITEEA (International Technology and Engineering Educators Association). 2000. Standards for Technological Literacy: Content for the Study of Technology. Reston, VA.

Keefe, B. 2009. The Perception of STEM: Analysis, Issues and Future Directions. Entertainment and Media Communication Institute, Division of Entertainment Industries Council, Inc. (EIC). Burbank, CA: EIC.

NAE (National Academy of Engineering). 2010. Standards for K–12 Engineering? Available at www.nap.edu/catalog.php?record_id=12990 (retrieved August 15, 2013).

NAE and NRC (National Research Council). 2009. Engineering in K–12 Education: Understanding the Status and Improving the Prospects. Washington: National Academies Press.

NAE and NRC. 2002. Technically Speaking: Why All Americans Need to Know More About Technology. Available at www.nap.edu/catalog.php?record_id=10250 (retrieved August 15, 2013).

NGACPB (National Governors Association Center for Best Practices). 2010. Common Core State Standards for Mathematics. Available at www.corestandards.org/assets/CCSSI_Math%20Standards.pdf (retrieved January 14, 2014).

NCMSTC (National Commission on Mathematics and Science Teaching for the 21st Century). 2000. Before It's Too Late: A Report to the Nation from the National Commission on Mathematics and Science Teaching for the 21st Century. Available at www.ptec.org/document/ServeFile.cfm?ID=4059&DocID=2813 (retrieved August 14, 2013).

NCTM (National Council of Teachers of Mathematics). 1989. Curriculum and Evaluation Standards for School Mathematics. Reston, VA.

NEA (National Education Association). 1894. Report of the Committee of Ten on Secondary School Studies: With the Reports of the Conferences Arranged by the Committee. New York: American Book Company. Available at http://books.google.com/books?id=PfcBAAAAYAAJ&pg=PA3&lpg=PA3#v=onepage&q&f=false (retrieved April 8, 2012).

NGA (National Governors Association). 2007. Innovation America: A Final Report. Available at www.nga.org/files/live/sites/NGA/files/pdf/0707INNOVATIONFINAL.PDF (retrieved August 14, 2013).

NRC. 1989. Everybody Counts: A Report to the Nation on the Future of Mathematics Education. Available at www.nap.edu/catalog.php?record_id=1199 (retrieved August 15, 2013).

NRC. 1996. National Science Education Standards. Washington: National Academy Press. Available at www.nap.edu/catalog.php?record_id=4962 (retrieved July 23, 2013).

NRC. 2007a. Rising Above the Gathering Storm: Energizing and Employing America for a Brighter Economic Future. Available at www.nap.edu/catalog.php?record_id=11463 9 (retrieved August 14, 2013).

NRC. 2007b. Taking Science to School: Learning and Teaching Science in Grades K-8. Washington: National Academies Press. Available at www.nap.edu/catalog.php?record_id=11625 (retrieved October 29, 2013).

NRC. 2009a. A New Biology for the 21st Century: Ensuring the United States Leads the Coming Biology Revolution. Washington: National Academies Press. Available at www.nap.edu/catalog.php?record_id=12764 (retrieved July 23, 2013).

NRC. 2009b. Learning Science in Informal Environments: People, Places, and Pursuits. Washington: National Academies Press. Available at www.nap.edu/catalog.php?record_id=12190 (retrieved October 29, 2013).

NRC. 2012a. A Framework for K–12 Science Education: Practices, Crosscutting Concepts, and Core Ideas. Washington: National Academies Press. Available at www.nap.edu/catalog.php?record_id=13165 (retrieved July 17, 2013).

NRC. 2012b. Discipline Based Education Research: Understanding and Improving Learning in Undergraduate Science and Engineering. Washington: National Academies Press. Available at www.nap.edu/catalog.php?record_id=13362 (retrieved October 29, 2013).

NSB (National Science Board). 2007. National Action Plan for Addressing the Critical Needs of the U.S. Science, Technology, Engineering and Mathematics Education System. Available at www.nsf.gov/nsb/documents/2007/stem_action.pdf (retrieved August 14, 2013).

NSF (National Science Foundation). 2012. Science and Engineering Indicators. State graduation requirements for mathematics and science, by number of years required: Selected years, 1987–2008. Available at www.nsf.gov/statistics/seind12/c1/tt01-06.htm (retrieved July 17, 2013).

OSTP (Office of Science and Technology Policy). 2011. The Federal Science, Technology, Engineering, and Mathematics (STEM) Education Portfolio: A Report from the Federal Inventory of STEM Education Fast-Track Action Committee, Committee on STEM Education, National Science and Technology Council. Available at www.whitehouse.gov/sites/default/files/microsites/ostp/costem__federal_stem_education_portfolio_report.pdf (retrieved April 4, 2012).

PCAST (President's Council of Advisors on Science and Technology). 2012. Report to the President. Engage to Excel: Producing One Million Additional College Graduates with Degrees in Science, Technology, Engineering and Mathematics. Available at www.whitehouse.gov/sites/default/files/microsites/ostp/pcast-engage-to-excel-final_feb.pdf (retrieved August 14, 2013).

Sanders, M. 2009. STEM, STEM education, STEMmania. The Technology Teacher, December/January, 20-26.

Stanic, G.M.A. and J. Kilpatrick, 1992. Mathematics curriculum reform in the United States: A historical perspective. International Journal of Educational Research 17:407–417.

2

A Descriptive Framework for Integrated STEM Education

The study committee was tasked with identifying and characterizing existing approaches to integrated STEM education. As explained in Chapter 1, in determining the scope of the charge, we emphasized "connections" between and among the STEM subjects.[1] Seen this way, integrated STEM education occupies a multidimensional space in the larger K–12 education landscape: Rather than a single, well-defined experience, it involves a range of experiences with some degree of connection. The experiences may occur in one or several class periods, or throughout a curriculum; they may be reflected in the organization of a single course or an entire school, or they may be presented in an after- or out-of-school activity.

Each variant of integrated STEM education suggests different planning approaches, resource needs, implementation challenges, and outcomes. In this chapter we present a *framework* (Figure 2-1) with four features: (1) *goals* of integrated STEM education, (2) *outcomes* of integrated STEM education, (3) the *nature and scope* of integrated STEM education, and (4) *implementation* of integrated STEM education. Each feature has specific subcomponents, as shown in Figure 2-1, thus providing a vocabulary for researchers, practitioners, and others to identify, describe, and investigate specific integrated STEM initiatives in the US K–12 education system. Boxes throughout the

---

[1] "Between and among" refers to connections between any two STEM subjects (e.g., most commonly math and science) and those among three or more.

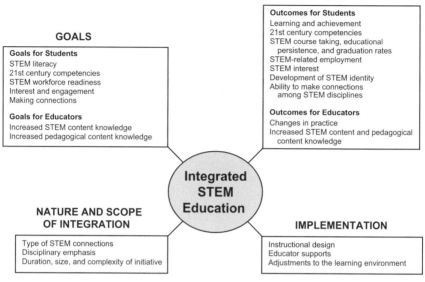

FIGURE 2-1 Descriptive Framework Showing General Features and Subcomponents of Integrated STEM Education

chapter briefly describe examples drawn from our review of selected programs and projects that illustrate the concepts discussed. Table 2-1 (see p. 48) shows use of the framework to characterize an integrated STEM education program. The committee used the framework to help clarify its thinking in writing the report; Chapters 5 and 6 mirror the framework's high-level structure. Chapter 3's analysis of the research focuses on two key outcomes described in the framework: those related to learning and achievement and those related to interest and identity.

The committee recognizes that numerous variables could be incorporated in a descriptive framework. In research involving 16 STEM schools, for example, Researchers Without Borders (2012) identified over 100 "critical components" deemed important to the schools' success. Our framework does not aim to be so comprehensive but rather to promote a more general, higher-level conceptualization of STEM education.

Although the framework treats the four features separately, they are meant to be interdependent in practice. These interdependencies are considered in Chapter 6 (Figure 6-1, Iterative Model of Educational Change).

GOALS OF INTEGRATED STEM EDUCATION

Goals are statements of what the developer of the particular educational intervention hopes to accomplish. The importance of attending to goals in the design of educational interventions cannot be overemphasized, as goals are the driver for an iterative process of educational change (see Fig. 6-1). Data gathered for the project revealed five major goals for students and two for educators:

Goals for Students

- STEM literacy
- 21st century competencies
- STEM workforce readiness
- Interest and engagement
- Ability to make connections among STEM disciplines

Goals for Educators

- Increased STEM content knowledge
- Increased pedagogical content knowledge

Some of these goals are quite high-level, such as encouraging more young people to enter STEM careers and increasing student interest in STEM subjects. Goals may also include more specific objectives, which are usually framed in a way that supports assessment (discussed in Chapter 5) of student learning or other outcomes. For example, an objective may be to provide students with learning experiences that support their ability to analyze how components of simple machines interact to produce desired outcomes).

In practice, goals and objectives are often used interchangeably, and some goals overlap. Many of the STEM programs and projects we examined claimed to address more than one goal, sometimes for both students and educators (Box 2-1). In some cases, goals seemed to serve more as indicators of general aspiration rather than as guides for the design and evaluation of programs, thus raising questions about the degree of focus on achieving goals as opposed to using them as statements of aspiration. Notwithstanding these complexities, it is important to try to identify the goals of a particular initiative; the absence of goals specified or even implied raises questions about the design of the initiative.

BOX 2-1
Example of Multiple Goals: CSTEM Challenge

The CSTEM (communications, science, technology, engineering, mathematics) Challenge is a year-long competition involving student teams across elementary, middle, and high schools. Its goals include:

- Empowering students to become innovators and technologically proficient problem solvers
- Increasing students' 21st century skills and STEM literacy
- Enriching community understanding of STEM education and its importance in building capacity to prepare students for work and life in the 21st century
- Increasing teacher capacity to deliver STEM content in grades pre-K–12
- Serving as a channel for connecting classroom learning with the business sector to improve students' college and career readiness skills

SOURCE: www.cstem.org.

STEM Literacy and 21st Century Competencies

Two high-level goals associated with integrated STEM education are STEM literacy and 21st century competencies.

STEM literacy is a relatively new idea that has not been well defined in literature or practice, although significant work has gone into elaborating aspects of literacy in the individual STEM disciplines (e.g., AAAS 1990; ITEEA 1996; NRC 1989). From these efforts it is possible to infer that STEM literacy might include some combination of (1) awareness of the roles of science, technology, engineering, and mathematics in modern society, (2) familiarity with at least some of the fundamental concepts from each area, and (3) a basic level of application fluency (e.g., the ability to critically evaluate the science or engineering content in a news report, conduct basic troubleshooting of common technologies, and perform basic mathematical operations relevant to daily life).

Twenty-first century competencies[2] are a blend of cognitive, interpersonal, and intrapersonal characteristics that may support deeper learning and knowledge transfer. Cognitive competencies include critical thinking and innovation; interpersonal attributes include communication, collaboration, and responsibility; and intrapersonal traits include flexibility, initiative, and metacognition.

STEM Workforce Readiness

One goal of integrated STEM education is the development of a STEM-capable workforce. Efforts to achieve this goal may focus on increasing the number of individuals who (1) develop STEM skills through school-to-work, tech prep, or career and technical education (CTE) experiences in high school, (2) earn STEM-related degrees at the certificate, associate's, or bachelor's levels, equipping them for jobs such as K–12 STEM teachers, medical assistants, nurses, and computer and engineering technicians, or (3) pursue professional degrees[3] in one of the STEM fields. Such efforts may start at the high school level, as illustrated by the example in Box 2-2.

Interest and Engagement

Another frequently cited goal of integrated STEM education programs is to boost interest and engagement in the STEM subjects. Some programs stress STEM interest and engagement among all students; others focus on specific populations, such as those historically underrepresented in STEM fields (i.e., girls and certain minorities) (Box 2-3). Chapter 3 discusses what is known from research about engagement and the related concepts of motivation and persistence.

---

[2] We prefer the term "21st century competencies" to "21st century skills." The two are related, but the former is a more robust concept that has been elaborated in recent work by the National Research Council (2012a).

[3] For engineering, the first professional degree is at the bachelor's level; for most areas of science, mathematics, and technology, the first professional degree is generally at the master's level.

BOX 2-2
Example of Career-Focused Goals: Build IT

Build IT: Girls Building Information Technology Fluency Through Design is an after-school and summer curriculum for middle school girls. One goal of the program, jointly run by SRI International and Girls Inc., is to increase girls' interest in and desire to take high school algebra, geometry, and computer science courses in preparation for postsecondary STEM education and careers. The Build IT curriculum consists of six 10-week units (average 2.5 hours per week) over two years, as well as extensive professional development resources for informal, out-of-school-time educators and staff. The program also includes structured interactions between the participating students and IT professionals—research has found that these interactions encourage girls' interest in IT careers (Koch et al. 2010).

BOX 2-3
Example of Engaging Girls in STEM: TechBridge

TechBridge (www.techbridgegirls.org) is a yearlong after-school program for girls in grades 5–12 that seeks to promote participants' interests and skills in science, technology, and engineering. The program provides hands-on activities and career exploration experiences, exposure to role models and mentoring, and field trips to STEM-focused enterprises. TechBridge began in the San Francisco Bay area and expanded to other parts of the country through a collaboration with the Girl Scouts. Research on the program has examined the importance of (1) social relationships and racial diversity in encouraging engagement (Kekelis et al. 2005) and (2) role models in shaping girls' interest in STEM subjects (Kekelis and Wei 2009).

Ability to Make Connections among STEM Disciplines

Integrated STEM education calls for making connections across disciplines, so it is important to develop student and educator awareness of these connections and to leverage the connections in ways that improve learning. For example, an understanding of the general idea of systems may be aided by examining electrical systems, mechanical systems, ecosystems, and even mathematical systems to identify their common characteristics.

Connections may also depend on a synthesis of approaches from multiple disciplines to yield understanding of a core concept or big idea, resulting in knowledge that is more integrated, wider in scope, or more differentiated than is typical of understandings developed within the boundaries of an individual discipline.

The committee's review of integrated STEM education programs found surprisingly few in which the goal of making connections was stated explicitly. But the design of many instructional materials and data from research and evaluation studies suggest that implied goals for students learning related to connections underlie many integrated STEM initiatives, as illustrated in the following competencies:

- recognizing and applying concepts that have different meanings or applications across disciplinary contexts (i.e., transfer);
- engaging in a STEM practice, such as engineering design, that uses knowledge from a different discipline, such as mathematics;
- combining practices from two or more STEM disciplines (e.g., scientific experimentation and engineering design) to solve a problem or complete a project;
- recognizing when a concept or practice is presented in an integrated way; and
- drawing on disciplinary knowledge to support integrated learning experiences and knowing when to do so.

Educator-Specific Goals

Some integrated STEM education programs target in-service teachers rather than or in addition to students, often through professional development activities tied to a specific curriculum. Goals for these programs frequently aim to build teachers' knowledge of subject-matter and pedagogical content knowledge relevant both to individual STEM subjects and to making connections between and among them (Box 2-4).

A related goal is to boost educators' pedagogical skills in subjects to which they may have had little exposure. This is especially true for professional development programs targeted to afterschool educators, who typically have little coursework in mathematics, science, or engineering (Klenk et al. 2012).

BOX 2-4
Example of Building Teacher Content
Knowledge: Everyday STEM

The goal of Everyday STEM is to help K–5 teachers integrate STEM into what they already do in their classrooms. The program was designed by a group of Virginia-based elementary technology education teachers who believe that the hands-on learning made possible by engineering design activities will "encourage children of all learning styles and abilities to develop ownership of the essential knowledge expected of elementary students in our rapidly changing world." The program provides teachers with instructional materials (from Pitsco) as well as a professional development course offered through the Content Teaching Academy of James Madison University. The course is intended to help teachers use design, engineering, and technology instructional resources to enhance children's attainment of the Virginia Standards of Learning in science, mathematics, social studies/history, and language arts.

SOURCES: www.pitsco.com, www.jmu.edu/contentacademy/Engineering.shtml, www.childrensengineering.com.

OUTCOMES OF INTEGRATED STEM EDUCATION

Education goals are closely related to outcomes. That is, a successful intervention should be tied to outcomes (or evidence) consistent with its goals. Our review of the literature and programs revealed six important outcomes for students and two for educators.

Outcomes for Students

- Learning and achievement
- 21st century competencies
- STEM course taking, educational persistence, and graduation rates
- STEM-related employment
- STEM interest, development of STEM identity
- Ability to transfer understanding across STEM disciplines

Outcomes for Educators

- Changes in practice
- Increased STEM content knowledge and pedagogical content knowledge

In reality, outcomes for some goals are difficult or impractical to measure. STEM literacy is a case in point. Because it has not yet been well defined and because it includes many different elements (see, for example, Bybee 2010), measuring STEM literacy as an outcome of a particular integrated educational experience can be problematic. However, individual aspects of STEM literacy—for example, understanding of specific science or mathematics concepts (Box 2-5) or awareness of how the STEM disciplines help shape our world—are measurable outcomes.

Similarly, development of 21st century competencies is a high-level goal with multiple components, such as improved communication or collaboration, and outcomes are likely to be tied to those individual components rather than to the overall concept.

In developing the framework the committee recognized that outcomes may be cognitive or affective, may reflect educational persistence, or may be some combination of these. Typically, cognitive outcomes are determined through standard measures of achievement, such as large-scale (e.g., state, national, or international) assessment; they may also be gauged through for-

---

BOX 2-5
Example of Understanding Science Concepts:
Engineering is Elementary

Developers of the Engineering is Elementary (EiE) curriculum at the Museum of Science, Boston, have conducted research to determine whether and to what extent students participating in the program increase their knowledge of science concepts as a result of engaging in engineering design activities. For example, in a unit on designing lighting systems, EiE researchers found that students significantly increased their understanding of concepts related to the properties of light, such as reflection, transmission, and absorption (Lachapelle et al. 2011).

mative or summative tests designed to measure learning related to a specific curriculum, course sequence, or activity.

In addition, interest is growing in the idea of assessing 21st century competencies such as flexible learning, ability to work with unstructured problems, communication, and teamwork as indicators of STEM learning (NRC 2012a). However, low-cost, valid, and reliable measures of these important competencies are not yet available (NRC 2012b).

Affective measures consider factors such as interest in or motivation to learn about STEM subjects as well as the development of a "STEM identity," a measure of the degree to which STEM subjects and careers are personally relevant to the learner. Efforts to study outcomes related to STEM identity have focused on single subjects (Box 2-6) rather than the broader concept of STEM. Educational persistence reflects how successfully and for how long an individual pursues STEM-related studies. Measures may include high school course taking (beyond the classes required by state law) and graduation rates, declared intended major, postsecondary STEM course taking, and matriculation in a STEM-related postsecondary degree program (Maltese and Tai 2011).

The discussion in Chapter 3 of research on integrated STEM learning and thinking makes clear that there are significant methodological and design weaknesses that limit the committee's ability to draw strong conclusions about outcomes of integrated STEM education. Part of the problem relates to the fact that some measured outcomes are not clearly connected to the intervention. In other cases, the design of the research itself may not allow inferences about outcomes. Suggestions for addressing some of these

---

BOX 2-6
Example of Boosting Interest in Mathematics:
Bedroom Design Activity

Researchers at the Hofstra University Center for Technological Literacy have tested the impact of introducing a mathematics-infused engineering and technology education curriculum on student attitudes toward mathematics. Mathematics concepts addressed in the activity included geometric shapes, factoring, percentages, scale, mathematical nets, and the computation of pricing information. The researchers found that students who studied mathematics as part of a computer-based bedroom design activity thought mathematics was more important and interesting in the context of technology than their counterparts in a control group who learned math in a traditional technology education class (Burghardt et al. 2010).

BOX 2-7
Example of Reducing Math Anxiety:
MST Teacher Education Program

In 1998, The College of New Jersey inaugurated a K–5 teacher education program that combines coursework in mathematics, science, and technology (MST) with instruction in pedagogy. One intriguing finding is that the MST students, who begin the program with relatively high levels of math anxiety, have much less anxiety—comparable to that of TCNJ math majors—after taking certain MST math classes. In contrast, math anxiety among non-STEM majors taking these same math courses remained relatively high (O'Brien 2010). The program's leaders believe these data may be explained by the initiative's interdisciplinary approach.

---

shortcomings are addressed in Chapter 6, which outlines directions for future research. Despite the current paucity of outcomes data for STEM education initiatives, we believe it is important that the framework include outcomes, if only to bring attention to the importance of designing integrated STEM experiences in a way that enables measurement of their impact on students.

The framework accounts for the fact that many educators likely will be impacted by integrated STEM education, in both preservice and in-service settings. Outcomes for educators will be reflected in changes in practices (e.g., the adoption or increased use of teaching strategies that support student engagement with science inquiry or engineering design); in expectations for their knowledge of subject-matter or pedagogical content; or in gains in teacher efficacy. Educator outcomes also might include an increase in student interest in STEM subjects (Box 2-7) or in the development of STEM-related identity among students.

NATURE AND SCOPE OF INTEGRATION

In examining the research literature and selected examples of integrated STEM initiatives, the committee identified three important elements that determine the nature and scope of integration:

- type of STEM connections,
- disciplinary emphasis, and
- duration, size, and complexity of initiative.

Regarding the nature of connection, integrated STEM education may bring together concepts from more than one discipline (e.g., mathematics and science, or science, technology, and engineering); it may connect a concept from one subject to a practice of another, such as applying properties of geometric shapes (mathematics) to engineering design; or it may combine two practices, such as science inquiry (e.g., doing an experiment) and engineering design (in which data from a science experiment can be applied).

In integrated STEM education it is frequently the case that one STEM subject has a dominant role—the explicit or implicit focus of a project, program, or school is to develop students' knowledge or skill mainly in one content area, such as mathematics (Box 2-8). The inclusion of concepts or practices from other subjects is often intended to support or deepen learning and understanding in the targeted subject.

In terms of scope, integrated STEM education initiatives exhibit a variety of relevant parameters, such as duration, setting, size, and complexity. Initiatives may occur as a single hour-long project or over one or several class periods, or they may be reflected in the organization of a single course, a multicourse curriculum, or an entire school. Most of the programs we examined have very small footprints, existing as pilot efforts involving just a few students. But some have been implemented much more broadly, sometimes across several schools or states, engaging hundreds or thousands of participants.

BOX 2-8
Example of a Dominant Discipline in STEM Integration:
MathAlive!

MathAlive! (www.mathalive.com) is a 5,000-square-foot traveling exhibit that presents mathematics in the context of real-world applications. It is underwritten by Raytheon and was developed in partnership with the National Council of Teachers of Mathematics, NASA, the National Society of Professional Engineers, MATHCOUNTS, and the Society of Women Engineers. The connections between math and the other STEM disciplines are explicit in the design of the exhibit interactives. For example, in "Easy on the Gas," visitors are challenged to use systems engineering to create a mathematical simulation that relieves traffic gridlock and reduces fuel consumption. In "Ramp It Up," visitors explore simple machines and design specifications to design a skateboard that can perform a specific trick.

Complexity varies, too, from efforts that are designed to be plugged in to an established curriculum (with no other changes to the status quo) to those that ambitiously strive to design a new integrated learning experience in concert with professional development for the teachers who will deliver it, sometimes in the context of a whole-school design. Some efforts do this and more, including building in a component of research or evaluation.

Finally, as illustrated in the examples presented in this chapter and elsewhere in the report, considerable efforts are being made to expose young people to integrated STEM education experiences in settings outside the formal classroom.

The scope and nature of integration have a direct bearing on the time and resources needed for implementation; on the level of acceptance or resistance such initiatives receive from students, educators, and administrators; and on the types of outcomes that may be expected and the challenge of measuring them.

IMPLEMENTATION

A range of factors must be considered in the implementation of integrated STEM education. The committee focuses here on three:[4]

- instructional design,
- educator supports, and
- adjustments to the learning environment.

Regarding instructional design, the programs we reviewed included a variety of approaches to teaching, from traditional, highly structured direct instruction to methods that are more student centered, experiential, and open ended, often involving variants of problem-based learning (Box 2-9).

Engineering design (Box 2-10), like problem-based learning (PBL), is associated with a large number of efforts to teach the STEM subjects in an integrated fashion. Science inquiry, engineering design, and PBL share features that can provide students with opportunities to apply STEM concepts and engage in STEM practices in interesting and relevant contexts.

By educator supports, we mean the opportunities provided to STEM educators to improve STEM content knowledge and pedagogical practices

---

[4] Additional factors related to implementing integrated STEM education are addressed in Chapter 5.

BOX 2-9
Problem-Based Learning and Integrated STEM Education

Problem-based learning, or PBL, is an experiential instructional strategy that encourages students to be active learners by engaging them in loosely structured problems that resemble situations they might encounter in their lives and for which multiple solutions are possible. Though not synonymous with or required for connected STEM learning, many STEM integration initiatives examined by the committee used some form of PBL. The central features of PBL, according to Barrows (1996), are

- student centeredness,
- small group work,
- teachers as facilitators or guides,
- problems as both the focus and stimulus for learning, and
- acquisition of new information through self-directed learning.

Other instructional designs, particularly project-based learning, share many of these traits, thus the terms *problem-based* and *project-based* learning are often confused or used interchangeably. Other terms sometimes associated with PBL-type instruction are *authentic, real-world, challenge-based,* and *concrete,* and each appears in the literature describing integrated STEM education.

Readers wishing more detail about problem- and project-based learning strategies may want to consult one or more of the following: Barron et al. 1998; Savery 2006; Strobel and van Barneveld 2009.

---

in ways that support subject-matter integration, typically through pre- and in-service professional development (Box 2-11).

Adjustments to the learning environment may entail extended class periods to allow students more time to repeat experiments or iterate and improve a design; extended lesson planning, team teaching, and other ways of developing a professional learning community (Box 2-12); or opportunities for partnering between STEM educators working in schools and those working outside schools, for example, in museums and higher-education institutions.

The factors discussed here are illustrative, not comprehensive. It is certainly appropriate to consider other factors in the implementation of integrated STEM education. For example, extensive research documents the importance of *fidelity of implementation* to the long-term success of educational innovations (e.g., O'Donnell 2008). Fidelity—the delivery of a

---

BOX 2-10
Engineering Design and Integrated STEM Education

The engineering design process, a problem-solving method, is used by engineers—along with knowledge from mathematics and science—to solve technical challenges. According to *Standards for Technological Literacy: Content for the Study of Technology* (ITEEA 2000), engineering design has a number of attributes.

First, it is purposeful; a designer begins with an explicit goal that is clearly understood; thus design can be pictured as a journey with a particular destination, rather than a sightseeing trip. Second, designs are shaped by *specifications* and *constraints*. Specifications spell out what the design is intended to accomplish. Constraints are limitations the designer must contend with, such as costs, size requirements, or the physical limitations of the materials used. In addition, the design process is systematic and iterative.

Engineering design can be a highly social and collaborative enterprise as well. Engineers engaged in design activities often work in teams and communicate with clients and others.

In K–12 education, engineering design has come to be seen as the central practice for students engaged in engineering activities (NAE and NRC 2009; NRC 2012b). The words and phrases used by different integrated STEM education efforts to describe the process vary, but the basic approaches are analogous and generally include the following steps (although not necessarily in this order):

Identify the problem or objective
Define goals and identify the constraints
Research and gather information
Create potential design solutions
Analyze the viability of solutions
Choose the most appropriate solution
Build and implement the design
Test and evaluate the design
Repeat all steps as necessary
Communicate the results

Readers wishing more details about design-based learning strategies may want to consult Crismond and Adams 2012.

BOX 2-11
Example of Professional Development for Integration:
Idaho STEM Summer Institute

The Idaho STEM Summer Institute is a four-day residential experience for approximately 300 grade 4–9 teacher teams from across the state. The 32-hour program involves lectures, panels, field trips, and lab activities and includes 20 hours of content/domain-specific instruction. An evaluation of teacher engagement developed by researchers at Boise State University found, among other outcomes, that educators increased their purposeful coordination with instruction in other content areas as a result of their participation in the program (Nadelson et al. 2012).

---

curriculum or other educational intervention in a manner consistent with its original design—is critical to produce outcome measures that can inform decisions to continue, modify, or terminate a particular intervention.

At the same time, there is an argument that differences in local circumstances and priorities justify modification of some aspects of an intervention, particularly if it is an innovative one (Berman 1981; Dusenbury et al. 2003). A large-scale study of educational change efforts in five school districts gave

---

BOX 2-12
Example of Professional Learning Community:
Manor New Tech High School

Manor (Texas) New Technology High School (MNTHS) is one of over 100 schools in the New Tech Network (www.newtechnetwork.org), a nonprofit that supports project-based-learning approaches to education reform. Every Monday is a late start day for students while staff engage in professional development meetings and leadership committees. Teachers are encouraged to team teach across disciplines, and the school provides time for teachers to receive peer feedback on project designs and suggestions on how to adapt tactics as student projects progress. The school's Teacher Advancement Program System provides time and compensation for teachers to take on additional responsibilities and roles, such as providing assistance and mentorship for newer teachers. Each Manor teacher participates in a minimum of 150 hours of professional development annually (E3 Alliance 2009).

---

rise to the construct of *mutual adaptation*, which treats accommodations on the part of both the district and the organization delivering the educational intervention as both inevitable and, in many cases, desirable (Berman and McLaughlin 1976).

In all cases, careful documentation of implementation practices and program outcomes is needed to build understanding of the critical components of an innovation and to inform decisions about whether to continue programs.

USING THE FRAMEWORK

This framework will be useful to a variety of groups and for several purposes. It should enable administrators, teachers, curriculum developers, funders, and others to better understand what is a confusing and underresearched trend in the US education system. By clearly defining a small number of salient features, the framework can stimulate productive and meaningful discussion about efforts in the name of integrated STEM education.

The framework can be used to examine and compare features of programs that have characteristics of integrated STEM. Table 2-1 illustrates just such a characterization for an integrated STEM initiative examined by the committee.

The framework also will enable researchers in education and the cognitive sciences to start developing and testing hypotheses about the relationships among critical elements of integrated STEM education. For example, keeping other parameters constant, what might happen to student outcomes related to STEM identity when the nature of integration varies? As the framework is explored in this way and yields a better understanding of integrated STEM education, some underlying assumptions may prove not to be useful and the framework will need to be adjusted to account for new data. This is appropriate and desirable.

CONCLUSION

This chapter provides a relatively simple organizing scheme to help readers with a range of interests and expertise begin to make sense of integrated STEM education. The framework almost certainly will need to be revised as more is learned, through research and practice, about how the STEM subjects can be connected to support student learning and other outcomes.

TABLE 2-1 Integrated STEM in the Harrisonburg City Public School System, Harrisonburg, Virginia. Target population: Students K–12 with emphasis on elementary grades.

HIGH-LEVEL FEATURE	SUBCOMPONENT	RELEVANT DETAILS
Goals	STEM literacy	Target specific STEM skills in students and teachers
Nature of integration	S, T, E, and M	• Engages students in engineering design process as a way to study core content through a variety of challenges (e.g., studying simple machines to discover what makes an elevator work and the design of bird beaks for capturing different kinds of foods) • Addresses standards in science, technology, engineering, and mathematics
Implementation	Educator supports	• Uses STEM strategies developed at VA Tech; district STEM coordinator has modeled classroom activities in classes for teachers • Teachers provided with "proven units" during professional development sessions • Yearlong professional development provided for teachers • Teachers participate in developing research questions for design challenges
	Instructional approaches	Engineering design–based program brings together elements from S, T, E, and M in a series of design challenges at each grade level in elementary grades
Outcomes	Cross-subject competencies and identity change in students	Based on anecdotal evidence only, students: • improved at integrative learning • felt success and saw friends succeed
	STEM-related changes in teacher practice	Continual improvement of STEM model and lessons

REFERENCES

AAAS (American Association for the Advancement of Science). 1990. Science for all Americans. New York: Oxford University Press.

Barron, B.J.S., D.L. Schwartz, N.J. Vye, A. Moore, A. Petrosino, L. Zech, and J.D. Bransford. 1998. Doing with understanding: Lessons from research on problem- and project-based learning. The Journal of the Learning Sciences 7(3/4): 271–311. Available at http://links.jstor.org/sici?sici=1050–8406%281998%297%3A3%2F4%3C271%3ADWULFR%3E2.0.CO%3B2–2 (retrieved October 31, 2013).

Barrows, H.S. 1996. Problem-based learning in medicine and beyond: A brief overview. In L. Wilkerson and H. Gilselaers (Eds.), Bringing problem-based learning to higher education: Theory and practice (pp. 3–12). San Francisco, CA: Jossey-Bass.

Berman, P. 1981. Educational change: An implementation paradigm. In R. Lehming and M. Kane (Eds.), Improving schools: Using what we know (pp. 253–286). London, UK: Sage.

Berman, P., and M.W. McLaughlin. 1976. Implementation of educational innovations. The Educational Forum 40:345–370.

Burghardt, M.D., D. Hecht, M. Russo, J. Lauckhardt, and M. Hacker. 2010. A study of mathematics infusion in middle school technology education classes. Journal of Technology Education 22(1): 58–74.

Bybee, R. 2010. Advancing STEM education: A 2020 vision. Technology and Engineering Teacher 70(1):30–35.

Crismond, D.P., and R.S. Adams. 2012. The informed design teaching and learning matrix. Journal of Engineering Education 101(4):738–797.

Dusenbury, L., R. Brannigan, M. Falco, and W.B. Hansen. 2003. A review of research on fidelity of implementation: Implications for drug abuse prevention in school settings. Health Education Research 18(2):237–256.

E3 Alliance. 2009. Case study of New Manor High School: Promising practices for comprehensive high schools. Available at http://mnths.manorisd.net/ourpages/auto/2012/3/7/39399794/MNTHS_Case%20Study.pdf (retrieved July 17, 2013).

ITEEA (International Technology and Engineering Educators Association). 1996. Technology for all Americans: Rationale and structure for the study of technology. Reston, VA: ITEEA.

ITEEA. 2000. Standards for technological literacy: Content for the study of technology. Reston, VA: ITEEA.

Kekelis, L.S., R.W. Ancheta, E. Heber, and J. Countryman. 2005. Bridging differences: How social relationships and racial diversity matter in a girls' technology program. Journal of Women and Minorities in Science and Engineering 11(3):231–246.

Kekelis L.S., and J. Wei. 2009. Role models matter: Promoting career exploration in after-school programs. ITest white paper. Available at http://afterschoolconvening.itestlrc.edc.org/sites/afterschoolconvening.itestlrc.edc.org/files/ITEST_white_paper_10_Techbridge.pdf (retrieved January 15, 2013).

Klenk, P.A., G.A. Ybarra, and R.D. Dalton. 2012. Challenges of introducing engineering in after-school settings. Proceedings of the 2012 American Society for Engineering Education Annual Conference and Exposition. Available at http://search.asee.org/search/fetch?url=file%3A%2F%2Flocalhost%2FE%3A%2Fsearch%2Fconference%2FAC2012%2F4830.pdf&index=conference_papers&space=129746797203605791716676178&type=application%2Fpdf&charset= (retrieved January 15, 2013).

Koch, M., A. Georges, T. Gorges, and R. Fujii. 2010. Engaging youth with STEM professionals in afterschool programs. Meridian—A Kindergarten Through High School Information and Communication Technologies Journal. Available at www.ncsu.edu/meridian/winter2010/koch/index.htm (retrieved January 15, 2013).

Lachapelle, C.P., C.M. Cunningham, J. Jocz, A.E. Kay, P. Phadnis, J. Wertheimer, and R. Arteaga. 2011. Engineering is Elementary: An evaluation of years 4 through 6 field testing. Boston, MA: Museum of Science.

Maltese, A.V., and R.H. Tai. 2011. Pipeline persistence: The effects of school experiences on earning degrees in STEM. Science Education 95(5):877–907.

Nadelson, L.S., A. Seifert, A.J. Moll, and B. Coats. 2012. I-STEM summer institute: An integrated approach to teacher professional development in STEM. Boise State University, Boise, IN. ScholarWorks. Available at http://scholarworks.boisestate.edu/cgi/viewcontent.cgi?article=1092&context=cifs_facpubs (retrieved June 18, 2013).

NAE (National Academy of Engineering) and NRC (National Research Council). 2009. Engineering in K-12 Education: Understanding the Status and Improving the Prospects. Available at www.nap.edu/catalog.php?record_id=12635 (retrieved August 29, 2013).

NRC. 1989. Everybody counts: A report to the nation on the future of mathematics education. Washington: National Academy Press.

NRC. 2012a. Education for life and work: Developing transferable knowledge and skills in the 21st Century. Washington: National Academies Press. Available at www.nap.edu/catalog.php?record_id=13398 (retrieved September 25, 2012).

NRC. 2012b. Monitoring progress toward successful K–12 STEM education: A nation advancing? Washington: National Academies Press. Available at www.nap.edu/catalog.php?record_id=13509 (retrieved June 18, 2013).

O'Brien, S. 2010. A unique multi-disciplinary STEM K–5 teacher preparation program. Proceedings of the American Society for Engineering Education, Annual Conference and Exposition. Washington: ASEE.

O'Donnell, C. 2008. Defining, conceptualizing, and measuring fidelity of implementation and its relationship to outcomes in K–12 curriculum intervention research. Review of Educational Research 78(1):33–84.

Researchers Without Borders. 2012. Explore STEM school critical components. Chicago: The Center for Elementary Mathematics and Science Education, University of Chicago. Available at http://researcherswithoutborders.org/projects/understanding-stem-schools/components (retrieved October 12, 2012).

Savery, J.R. 2006. Overview of problem-based learning: Definitions and distinctions. Interdisciplinary Journal of Problem-based Learning 1(1). Available at http://dx.doi.org/10.7771/1541–5015.1002 (retrieved October 31, 2013).

Strobel, J., and A. van Barneveld. 2009. When is PBL more effective? A meta-synthesis of meta-analyses comparing PBL to conventional classrooms. Interdisciplinary Journal of Problem-based Learning, 3(1). Available at http://dx.doi.org/10.7771/1541–5015.1046 (retrieved October 31, 2013).

3

Integrated STEM Education Experiences: Reviewing the Research [1]

Many claims are made about the benefits to students' learning and thinking of integrating education across science, technology, engineering, and mathematics (STEM). In this chapter we explore the evidence relevant to whether and how integrated approaches to STEM education support a range of outcomes within and across the disciplines. The full range of outcomes was described in Chapter 2. Here, we consider two main types of outcomes: those related to learning and achievement and those related to interest and identity.

As noted in Chapter 2, integrated STEM instruction is typically accomplished through the use of problem-, project-, or design-based tasks to engage students in addressing complex contexts that reflect real-world situations. For example, students might be invited to build an oven that is environmentally friendly or functional in settings where people do not have access to electricity. The students would use the engineering process to create a solar oven and in doing so investigate a wide range of STEM concepts such as the thermal properties of materials and how density affects a material's performance as a thermal insulator. They might use mathematics for measuring, and for graphing and interpreting data, and even develop a mathematical model of device behavior to inform the process of design.

---

[1]This chapter is based on the literature review overseen by David Heil and Associates and on commissioned papers by Angela Calabrese Barton, Michigan State University, Mary Gauvain, University of California, Riverside, and K. Ann Renninger, Swarthmore College.

Through iterative design cycles the students would engage in planning, creating, testing, and improving their inventions.

As illustrated in this example, we define integration to mean working in the context of complex phenomena or situations on tasks that require students to use knowledge and skills from multiple disciplines.

LEARNING AND ACHIEVEMENT

Research on the impact of integrated experiences on students' achievement, disciplinary knowledge, problem-solving ability, and ability to make connections between domains is not extensive, and concerns related to both the design of studies and the reporting of results hamper the ability to make strong claims about the effectiveness of integrated approaches. Nonetheless, preliminary conclusions can be drawn from the well-designed studies. The findings suggest that integration can lead to improved conceptual learning in the disciplines but that the effects differ, depending on the nature of the integration, the outcomes measured, and the students' prior knowledge and experience.

Most studies of STEM learning consider each discipline singly and do not measure students' ability to make connections across disciplines or their proficiency with skills such as collaboration or general problem solving. In addition, learning is often assessed using standardized achievement tests, which may not effectively measure the full range of learning and reasoning outcomes supported by integrated experiences. Assessment instruments on integration are rare because theories and tests have generally focused on content area–specific concepts and procedures and because, as explained in Chapter 2, there is no widely accepted definition of integrative thinking.

Beyond these assessment challenges, there are fundamental conceptual difficulties as well. A major difficulty follows from the simple fact that disciplinary knowledge is structured—understanding disciplinary ideas depends on understanding how they fit with other, related ideas. Concepts make sense not as isolated facts but as elements of integrated bodies (or structures) of knowledge, and learning means developing or "building" those structures, often over extended spans of time.

Although education research has made some progress in understanding how to help students construct coherent bases of disciplinary knowledge, domain-general learning principles provide limited guidance. Instead, how to support the development of disciplinary knowledge remains largely an empirical enterprise, in which cycles of research and trials with students and teachers gradually yield information about the most fruitful starting points, what conceptual resources students bring, and the kinds of instruction that are needed. Because integrated knowledge structures are developed gradually, it takes time—weeks, months, or years—for researchers to track their growth of student knowledge. Consequently, information about how to best help students learn with understanding is still limited to relatively few topics and has not yet resulted in widespread changes in educational practices.

Given these difficulties, it is not surprising that very little is known about how to organize curriculum and instruction so that emerging knowledge in different disciplines will mesh smoothly and at the right time to yield the kind of integration that supports coherent learning. Without very careful attention to developing coherent knowledge structures, the danger is that one or more of the "integrated" disciplines will receive short shrift in its development.

Integrating Mathematics and Science

The most well-studied integrated STEM education pairing is that of mathematics and science (e.g., Berlin and Lee 2003, 2005; Czerniak et al. 1999; Hurley 2001; Pang and Good 2000), but the number of studies that report the effects of integration on student learning in these two subjects separately is small. Moreover, the studies often are not explicit about the theory guiding how learning in the two subjects is coordinated and developed. Czerniak and colleagues (1999) noted in a review of the literature that there were few empirical studies of the integration of mathematics and science; many of the published articles promoted assumed benefits of integration or were theoretical in nature. Yet among the few empirical articles, Czerniak and colleagues saw a general trend toward a positive influence of integration on science and mathematics learning, although they pointed out that the descriptions of integration were so impoverished that it is difficult to make generalizations about the different approaches described.

Hurley (2001) conducted a meta-analysis of 31 studies that compared integrated mathematics and science instruction to a nonintegrated control group and reported mathematics and/or science achievement measures. She found positive effects of integration on scores in both math (ES = .27)[2] and science (ES = .37), which is consistent with other meta-analyses that report small to medium positive effects of integration (Hartzler 2000), although the effects varied both by subject and by the year the study was conducted. The lowest overall effect size for math achievement (ES = .07) was observed in the 10 most recent studies reviewed (1980s–1990s) and was lower than the effect for science achievement in all time periods.

Hurley also separated the achievement results by the level of integration (as described in the study reports) using the following categories:

- *Sequenced*: science and mathematics are planned and taught sequentially, with one preceding the other.
- *Parallel*: science and mathematics are planned and taught simultaneously through parallel concepts.
- *Partial*: science and mathematics are taught partially together and partially as separate disciplines in the same classes.
- *Enhanced*: either science or mathematics is the major discipline of instruction, with the other discipline apparent throughout the instruction.
- *Total*: science and mathematics are taught together in intended equality.

The effect size for mathematics achievement was positive and large when using a sequenced integration model (for mathematics ES = .85, for science ES = .34) but much lower for all other models of integration, ranging from −.11 for parallel instruction to .20 for total integration; parallel instruction also produced a negative effect size in science (ES = −.09). Both enhanced instruction (.66) and total integration (.96) produced large positive effect sizes for science.

Hurley also examined the 31 studies by grade level. At the elementary level there was only one study that examined mathematics. At the middle school level, two studies had outcomes for both science and mathematics. At the high school level, six studies had science outcomes and four mathe-

---

[2] Effect size (ES) was calculated by subtracting the control group mean from the treatment group mean and dividing by the combined standard deviation of the treatment and control groups, following the recommendation of Hedges et al. (1989). Small effect sizes are around .3 or less, medium effect sizes around .5, and large effect sizes .8 or above. A negative effect size indicates that the traditional group outperformed the experimental group.

matics outcomes. At the college level, two studies had outcomes for science and three for mathematics.

At both the middle and high school levels the effect sizes for science were higher than those for mathematics, indicating that it may be difficult to enhance mathematics achievement by integrating the math into another disciplinary context. Similar results in an unpublished meta-analysis of math and science integration also suggest that there are fewer positive benefits of integration for mathematics outcomes compared to science outcomes (Hartzler 2000). One possible explanation is that attempts to integrate science ideas with ideas from mathematics may interrupt a sequential approach thought to help students investigate and elaborate the rich relations among mathematical concepts and procedures (Lehrer and Schauble 2000).

In contrast, Lehrer and Schauble (2006) found enhanced development of scientific concepts known to be challenging to students in the elementary grades when the students use mathematics as a resource for representing and modeling natural systems. These more carefully articulated studies of the use of mathematical systems as tools for learning about natural systems suggest that effect sizes may depend on details of the instructional approach that are obscured by simple characterizations of the temporal sequence of integration.

According to other studies, the nature of the mathematical tools and systems of representation available to students determine the depth and breadth of learning about core ideas in science because mathematical forms correspond to forms of understanding natural systems. For example, Sherin (2001) noted that university students' models of force and motion were bound with symbolic equations. When students worked with the relations among quantities expressed by equations, they occasionally generated novel equations that prompted elaboration and reconsideration of core concepts. DiSessa (2000) posits that new forms of mathematical expression supported by computational media can make new ways of understanding science and mathematics accessible to larger numbers of students. For example, studies of student learning about complex systems indicate that agent-based descriptions—descriptions that represent phenomena as a large collection of interacting individuals—support learning about phenomena that are traditionally difficult to learn, such as electricity (Sengupta and Wilensky 2011), statistical mechanics (Wilensky 2003), and natural selection and population dynamics (Dickes and Sengupta 2012; Wilensky and Reisman 2006).

Collectively, these studies suggest that the integration of mathematics and science can be supported by engaging students in the invention and revision of mathematical models of natural systems. A strong implication is that learning science entails learning to express the behavior of natural systems as mathematical models, making this form of integration not merely supportive of but indispensible to learning science.

Learning Science and Mathematics in the Context of Engineering Design[3]

Design-based approaches, a hallmark of engineering education, have received particular attention for their potential as a rich context for integrated STEM. The effect of engineering on learning in science and mathematics was examined in the NAE/NRC report *Engineering in K–12 Education* (2009). The authoring committee found preliminary but promising evidence of a positive impact of engineering on learning in science and mathematics. However, two published empirical studies of Project Lead the Way (PLTW), a major program in engineering education for middle and high schools, showed mixed results when state achievement test scores were the basis of comparison. In schools serving a high proportion of low-income families, all students showed significant overall gains in mathematics and science achievement scores between 8th and 10th grade regardless of their course enrollment. However, students enrolled in one or more PLTW engineering classes showed statistically less improvement in mathematics scores and a nonstatistical difference in science achievement scores over that period, compared with a control group (Tran and Nathan 2010a). In schools serving predominantly affluent families, PLTW students exhibited small gains in mathematics achievement but no improvement in science achievement compared with students in a control sample (Tran and Nathan 2010b).

The results of these two studies provide additional evidence that enhancing math achievement through integration with other disciplines is difficult to do, and it is likely that students need additional support in place to see how specific mathematics concepts and skills are integrated with the engineering activities in order to exhibit substantial gains in mathematics achievement. These studies also fail to show substantially larger gains for students participating in project-based engineering courses, underscoring the inconsistency in current research on integrated STEM instruction.

---

[3] This section is based in part on a commissioned paper by Petrosino et al. (2008) for the NAE/NRC Committee on Engineering Education K–12.

Other research has demonstrated the effectiveness of learning science concepts through design in some but not all situations (Baumgartner and Reiser 1997; Fortus et al. 2004; Mehalik et al. 2005, 2008; Penner et al. 1997, 1998; Sadler et al. 2000). This approach can be effective if concepts are introduced when students engage with the design activity (Baumgartner and Reiser 1997; Fortus et al. 2004; Mehalik et al. 2007) or when design failure provokes conceptual change as students redesign an artifact to meet a goal (Lehrer et al. 2008). In addition, participant structures such as research groups (Lehrer et al. 2008) and design sharing sessions (pinup sessions) (Kolodner 2002) can provide conversational forums for clarifying and elaborating relations between designed artifacts and scientific concepts. These collective forms of activity are described more fully in Chapter 4.

Studies reveal that students may not spontaneously make connections between the devices being designed and the related scientific concepts (Crismond 2001; Kozma 2003; Nathan et al. 2013) and that they tend to focus on aesthetic or ergonomic aspects of design (Crismond 2001; Penner et al. 1998). Connections between the representations and notation systems used for design and for science need to be made explicit to students (Fortus et al. 2004; Nathan et al. 2013), or the material must be presented in such a way that students grasp that they can invent and revise systems of representation to understand how a natural or designed system works. Furthermore, the scientific knowledge gained through design may be highly contextualized, unless the activities are developed to support transfer of knowledge from one context to another, for example by using designs that highlight similar concepts across contexts (Fortus et al. 2004, 2005).

Design can elicit naïve conceptions from students. Explaining how a device functions presents an opportunity for the exploration of appropriate scientific concepts, especially in the case of redesign. However, without instructional support nothing inherent in the design process will necessarily challenge students' ideas (Crismond 2001; Penner et al. 1997). Sadler and colleagues (2000) demonstrated the potential of redesign as an avenue to challenge naïve conceptions through rapid cycles of design activity that allow for many iterations to refine the student's understanding (see also Penner et al. 1997, 1998). Redesign may be particularly useful for instruction because many elements of the designed object are already working, and only a few need to be focused upon and changed (Crismond and Adams, 2012).

When students engage in an engineering design task, they are likely to develop contextually dependent ideas about designing (e.g., "rules of thumb" and "how-to" knowledge). At least initially, without instructional support, their design ideas are unlikely to connect to or be coherent with normative science ideas that might inform their designs.

Crismond (2001) showed that whereas experts recognize opportunities to connect with science ideas, nonexpert designers miss them. Even after lots of experience in given design contexts, individuals can reach an expert level but connect very different ideas to the context depending on their own conceptual frame. For example, aquarium hobbyists are likely to consider the practical challenges of designing an aquarium to support a specific range of aquatic organisms, whereas academic biologists may be more likely to focus on very general notions about how energy exchanges drive the system (Hmelo-Silver et al. 2007).

These findings highlight the need to carefully frame the instructional goals and settings to support students in making links to concepts in science. Box 3-1 provides an example of design as a context for integration.

A study of two elective digital electronics classes in two urban high schools examined instructional strategies that can support students in building connections across different representations of a phenomenon or situation when they are engaged in the complexities of design (Nathan et al. 2013). One classroom in each school was videotaped over 3 or 4 contiguous days; the participating students were in grades 10–12. In one school students participated in a unit on a voting booth security system; in the other they designed and built a digital circuit that tallied votes and passed resolutions only when a majority affirmed the resolution (with a tie favoring the vote of the president).

Analyses of the instructional moves made by the teachers and interactions between the teachers and students suggest that a key mechanism of integrated STEM education is cohesion of central concepts across the mathematics and science representations, engineering objects, design and construction activities, and social structures in the classroom. When cohesion was supported, students made useful connections across STEM disciplines, as was evident by their ability to move more fluidly among discipline-specific representations (e.g., Boolean algebraic expressions, schematized logic gates, and wiring of the digital circuits) and perform effective troubleshooting. Cohesion was effected through four pedagogical mechanisms:

1. identification of invariant relations and disciplinary concepts regardless of the surface features (Nathan et al. 2013);
2. coordination that "supports students' reasoning and meaning making by constructing clear links across representations and activities" (Nathan et al. 2013, p. 110);

BOX 3-1
Example of Using Design as a Context for Integration

In a study with 6th graders, the activity of designing vessels that float was used to make learning from experimentation more relevant to the students (Schauble et al. 1995). After being given a design brief, students individually constructed vessels and added weight until the vessel sank. They then graphed their vessel with others that had similar carrying capacities. This was followed by further individual work in which students drew designs from various views and reflected on their previous design in a journal. Working in teams, students negotiated their designs by experimenting with various aspects of them. These efforts were supplemented by teacher and whole-class discussions of concepts such as buoyancy and relative density. By synthesizing the data from the experimentation, students could go on to plan their final design.

During this activity across several classrooms, a number of instructional challenges emerged. Although reflection is critical to learning, it was difficult to balance reflection activities with time spent on the more dynamic portions of the design process. It was also difficult to keep students focused on the design rather than on diversions while still valuing their background knowledge. And it was challenging to ensure that students not only remained focused on their goal of making the best vessel but also understood how various aspects of design could lead to improvements.

Analysis of interviews with the students before and after the activity revealed that they learned science through design and showed an improved understanding of experimentation. It also revealed that from an instructional perspective it was important to change only one variable at a time. This was true even when variables that would not affect the outcome of an experiment were altered. Instances in which teachers substituted or altered one irrelevant variable (such as using different types of weights that look different but are the same weight) led to confusion for the students, who were still developing an understanding of experimental procedure. Furthermore, teachers rarely discussed patterns in data, assuming that they were obvious to the students; this was demonstrated not to be the case. Finally, students were not spontaneously aware of the value of examining the unsuccessful vessels for attributes to be excluded; this useful skill can be nurtured by explicitly drawing attention to it (Schauble et al. 1995).

This example highlights the importance of framing and instructional support in design activity for integrated STEM learning.

3. forward projection to orient students to connections between current events or representations and future ideas and activities, which "facilitates planning, highlights pending importance, and prepares students for future learning opportunities" (Nathan et al. 2013, p. 110); and

4. backward projection to previously encountered ideas and events, which "prompts students to engage in reflection and emphasizes making connections between new and prior knowledge" (Nathan et al. 2013, p. 110).

Learning Mathematics in the Context of Technology

Although evidence reviewed thus far indicates that it may be difficult to support mathematics learning in integrated contexts, at least two studies suggest it can be done when explicit attention is given to mathematics learning.

Stone and colleagues (2008) studied mathematics-enhanced career and technical education (CTE) courses in high school that covered multiple occupational contexts—business and marketing, auto technology, health and information technology, and agriculture (but *not* engineering). CTE teachers were randomly assigned to teach courses either with enhanced mathematics or using traditional approaches. The teachers in the enhanced courses received guidance on how to structure their classes and additional professional development and were partnered with a mathematics teacher. They provided explicit opportunities for students to focus on the mathematics concepts, rather than just using math in the occupational context. Students in the two courses performed at similar levels in terms of technical skills, but those in the math-enhanced courses did better on measures of general math ability compared to students in the regular technical education courses.

A study of efforts to "infuse" mathematics in a 20-day middle school engineering/technology (ETE) course (referenced in Chapter 2) also showed promising results (Burghardt et al. 2010).[4] Mathematics concepts and skills were introduced in the ETE curriculum at critical points through focused lessons to facilitate students' ability to make connections between the disciplines. The mechanism used was a bedroom design activity, engaging students in the planning, design, and physical modeling of a "bedroom" that must meet specific cost and building requirements (e.g., the window

---

[4] Infusion (the term used by the study authors) is similar to the enhanced approach to integration described by Hurley (2001).

area must be at least 20 percent of the floor area, the minimum room size is 120 square feet, the minimum closet size is 8 square feet). Eighth-grade students from 13 middle schools participated in the curriculum. Each teacher involved in the infusion curriculum was compared with a teacher in a "business as usual" technology class.

Students in both the infusion and comparison classrooms completed an assessment of mathematics concepts that were relevant to the bedroom design unit before and after instruction in the unit. Students in the infusion classes showed greater gains in scores from pre- to post-test than those in the control classes. It is important to point out, though, that the concepts on the mathematics test were closely aligned to the bedroom design unit and it is not clear from the study whether the students in the comparison classrooms were exposed to these concepts.

In a recent analysis of nationally representative data from the Education Longitudinal Study of 2002, Bozick and Dalton (2013) explored the effects of enrollment in CTE courses on mathematics achievement. Controlling for the characteristics of the students' background and those of the school or district, the authors found that enrollment in occupational courses did not compromise mathematics achievement when such courses were taken instead of academic courses. When examined alone, engineering and technology courses—a subset of occupational courses that the authors say incorporate quantitative skills, problem solving, and logic—were unrelated to mathematics achievement.

Learning about Engineering and Technology

Very few studies have examined outcomes related to understanding engineering and technology, but pilot studies conducted as part of a large-scale curriculum intervention in New Jersey show some promising results.

Engineering Our Future New Jersey (EOFNJ) is a collaborative effort of Stevens Institute of Technology, the New Jersey Department of Education, the National Center for Technological Literacy (NCTL) at the Museum of Science, Boston, and others to bring exemplary technology and engineering curricula, such as *Engineering is Elementary* (EiE) and *A World in Motion*, to mainstream New Jersey K–12 education. The goal of EOFNJ is to ensure that within the next five years all K–12 students in New Jersey experience engineering curricula with a focus on innovation, as a required component of their elementary, middle, and high school education. Pilot studies were conducted at each school level.

At the elementary level, two modules from the EiE curriculum were implemented in 13 schools. One module focused on water quality, and students designed a water filter. The second focused on wind energy, and students designed a windmill that could lift a small weight. Results of tests administered before and after indicate that students improved in their ability to identify examples of technology and in their knowledge of water filters, filter materials, the science involved with the water filter module, and windmills and blade materials.

At the next level, 11 middle schools implemented a 4-week module from *A World in Motion* that involved designing a simple, mechanically propelled toy. Results on before-and-after tests of students' conceptions of engineering and technology indicate that they improved their understanding of engineering.

At the high school level, 11 teachers from 10 high schools implemented 2 modules from the NCTL curriculum *Engineering the Future: Designing the World of the 21st Century* (NCTL 2005). One module was on fluid and thermal systems and included redesign of a boat to improve an aspect of the design. The second involved electrical and communication systems in which students worked with snap circuits. Results on pre-/posttests showed improvement in students' understanding of fluid and thermal systems and of electrical circuits.

Summary

The studies reviewed indicate that the integration of STEM concepts in applied settings can yield increased conceptual learning in the disciplines but that there remain too many inconsistencies and gaps to effectively implement or assess integrated STEM programs.

For example, the positive impact on learning appears to differ for science and mathematics—it is less evident for mathematics outcomes. For both science and mathematics, the impact on learning and achievement varies depending on the approach to integration and the kinds of supports both embedded in the task and provided through instruction. Integration shows improved results on assessments of specific concepts related to the intervention, but not on general mathematics or science achievement tests like those administered by states.

Furthermore, the evidence presented above has several limitations that need to be considered when identifying directions for future research and development. One of the most significant is the lack of a commonly agreed-upon definition for integration. Without one, it is difficult to consistently describe pedagogy or compare results across studies to develop a nuanced picture of whether and how different approaches to integration support learning. Likewise, without a common set of measures or criteria for documenting integrated learning, there is no clear basis on which to compare results. Moreover, there are few direct measures of integration as a construct or of outcomes that show how well students are able to make connections across disciplines. In the absence of standardized measures of integrated learning, researchers may use assessment instruments that are biased in favor of the particular intervention being studied, thus calling into question the validity of measures of STEM integration.

Finally, the research base includes a relatively small number of studies, with limited samples and often with potential problems with selection bias (e.g., only students who already do well in STEM or are interested in STEM participate). Studies span multiple age groups, include a variety of measures of learning or achievement, and effect sizes are generally small. In order to advance research on integrated STEM education, researchers need to consider a range of designs and methodological approaches. These are discussed in more detail in Chapter 6.

INTEREST AND IDENTITY

Fostering the development of students' interest and identity in STEM is an important potential outcome of integrated STEM experiences. Interest and identity are thought to lead to continued engagement in STEM-related activities as reflected in course selection and choice of out-of-school activities, college major, and career path. In this section we review the evidence to determine whether and how integrated approaches support the development of interest and identity and lead to continued engagement in STEM fields. The committee found that out-of-school programs or experiences emphasized these outcomes, whereas school-based programs were more likely to focus on achievement outcomes. In both types of settings, however, direct measures of interest and identity were infrequent, although there was somewhat more attention to continued engagement (e.g., course taking or career aspirations).

In the following sections we explain how interest and identity have been defined by researchers and describe the ways they have been explored in research. Next we examine evidence indicating whether integrated STEM experiences support the development of students' interest and identity in STEM.

What Are Interest and Identity?

Interest develops over time, beginning with the triggering of attention and extending to voluntary reengagement, often characterized in terms of curiosity, persistence, and resourcefulness (Hidi and Renninger 2006; Renninger and Hidi 2011). Research findings clearly show that the presence of interest positively affects learner attention, goals, and levels of learning (see Hidi and Renninger 2006; Renninger and Hidi 2011) and that learners of all ages can be supported to develop interest (see Renninger 2010).

Interest is also related to other outcomes that can influence learning such as self-efficacy, an individual's sense that s/he can be successful in a given domain. With more developed interest, the learner often has stronger feelings of self-efficacy and can better self-regulate behaviors to persevere on challenging tasks (Hidi and Ainley 2008; Sansone 2009).

Once an interest begins to develop, it can be sustained through instruction and/or out-of-school experiences, during which the learner often comes to identify with those who represent and pursue the interest professionally (Krapp 2007; Renninger 2009).

Identity generally refers to who one is or wants to be, as well as to how one is recognized by others—as a particular kind of person, with particular interests, expertise, and ways of being in particular social contexts, such as the classroom. Identity with respect to STEM has implications for how or why one might engage in classes, enroll in STEM courses, or use ideas and practices from STEM disciplines outside the classroom.

People have multiple shifting identities based on the diverse contexts and communities they encounter. As they move through time and space, they create, through their talk, actions, and interactions, different stories or narratives about who they are and want to be. These identities are always under negotiation, are contingent on the resources one has access to, and are shaped by a person's social, cultural, and historical context, both in the moment and over time (Holland et al. 2001; Wortham 2006). These complexities are illustrated in the case study of a middle school student, Chantelle, presented in Box 3-2.

BOX 3-2
Case Study of Identity Development in STEM

Because identities are always in the making and socially negotiated, they are difficult to isolate or to name, raising questions about how to study them and what role they might play in helping an individual make sense of best practices for integrating learning in STEM.

Take, for example, the case of Chantelle (see Calabrese Barton et al. 2012). In the 6th grade, Chantelle, a soft-spoken African American girl growing up as the only daughter of a single mother, disappeared from view in science class. She infrequently volunteered in class and her average grades made her neither a concern nor an interest of her teacher. She had an avid desire to be a dancer when she grew up and pursued all the dance-related opportunities available at her arts-based public magnet school. She had little interest in science and mathematics; she'd never met an engineer and did not know what they did. And yet, at the very time when interest and motivation to pursue STEM drops precipitously, especially among girls, Chantelle's interest—and scholastic achievement—in science increased. By 8th grade, she declared her interest in science and mathematics and stated her career goal to be a green architect, bringing together her love of the arts with science and engineering.

Why is it that Chantelle's interest in science increased and her identity in science developed into one of a confident and competent student of STEM? There is clear evidence that one reason for the change was her participation in a technology-rich science and engineering club grounded in project- and place-based approaches. She had joined the club because her friends were involved, and initially her participation mirrored that in the science classroom: She arrived on time and finished her work, but she talked only with her small peer group and appeared more interested in watching YouTube videos of singers and dancers than in the science at hand.

However, through a series of events, Chantelle's participation began to change. The turning point was her involvement in an after-school lightbulb audit at her school. Near the end of a unit on energy efficiency, Chantelle and two of her friends developed a project to determine how much energy and money their school was wasting by using incandescent lightbulbs. Saving money was important to them as budget cuts at their school loomed. They counted the number of incandescent bulbs in the school, documented their kilowatt-hour expenditure, and calculated how much money and CO_2 emissions would be saved if they replaced those

continued

BOX 3-2 Continued

bulbs with CFLs. They used a video recorder to document the process and to interview teachers and students on the topic. Chantelle's two friends led the effort, organized the spreadsheet, and made the suggestions for where to go in the building; Chantelle pointed to the lightbulbs in each video shot.

Chantelle's role changed, however, when the girls began to edit the video into a short documentary. She directed the editing, choreographed each new scene, and added text and graphics to pull out the message. As the group began to run out of time to finish the movie, Chantelle edited the film in her spare time. The project took about 6 weeks.

The lightbulb audit received such rave reviews by peers in the club that the girls were persuaded to seek permission to present their findings to their school's student congress and school leaders. When the local electric company got word of the video from the school principal, it donated 1000 CFLs for the youth to distribute to their peers at school.

Furthermore, Chantelle asked to present the project to her science class, a level of active participation that stood in stark contrast to her previous everyday participation. Not only did she present the material, she engaged the class by asking her peers questions about why they should care about lightbulbs. She positioned herself both as the expert and as someone who cares about her fellow students and about the connections between science and their world. The following school year, when her 7th-grade class studied energy transformations, Chantelle eagerly volunteered in class discussion. She became deeply engaged in her science class across a variety of lessons and was described by her teacher as someone he wishes he could "clone."

Chantelle's story is illustrative of one of the more positive identity pathways Calabrese Barton and her collaborators have observed among middle school youth. Her experience shows that identity work is ongoing and cumulative and can be either facilitated or constrained by opportunities in the spaces where a student encounters science.

This case study also vividly illustrates the role of integrated STEM experiences and place- and project-based learning in fostering a productive science identity, which in turn enabled greater participation in the classroom, greater opportunities to learn, and the sense that a future in science is possible. Had the researchers only studied Chantelle's achievement, or only studied her at a moment in time, they would have missed her developmental pathway.

Many studies of identity in STEM disciplines have been tied, in some form, to concerns about equity, in the context of underrepresentation and as a factor in pipeline losses. Studies have documented K–12 classroom and school practices that may contribute to certain students' choices to disengage from STEM, such as African American girls (Calabrese Barton et al. 2012) who felt they had to choose friendships over extracurricular science in order to make academic success acceptable. Brown (2004, 2006) similarly observed that students "disidentified" with science to avoid cultural conflict.

Identity research may also help to explain why some instructional reforms succeed or fail even when they take into account gender, race, and language concerns (e.g., Carlone et al. 2011).

Evidence that Integrated STEM Supports Development of Interest and Identity

In addition to the case study illustrated in Box 3-2, evaluations of and research on integrated STEM programs provide preliminary evidence that such programs support the development of interest, identity, and continuation in STEM. As noted, however, measures of interest and of continuation in STEM are more common in studies of out-of-school programs, and in most cases the outcomes are measured without careful attention to the specific mechanisms that support the development of interest. Documentation of the development of identity is less common, and the few studies that have examined it in the context of integrated STEM are qualitative.

Interest

Studies and evaluations reviewed by the committee provide some evidence that integrated STEM programs can support the development and maintenance of interest in STEM. The programs or interventions considered were school-based projects and curriculum units, afterschool programs, and summer camps.

The study by Burghardt and colleagues (2010) of the infusion of mathematics into an ETE curriculum for middle school students (described in the previous section) documented outcomes related to interest. Students in the infusion curriculum and those in a comparison curriculum completed surveys of their attitudes toward mathematics and technology both before and after the intervention. Survey questions assessed the students' interest in mathematics and their perceptions of the importance of mathematics for technology and the relevance of mathematics. Comparison of the postsurvey responses of the two groups showed that students in the mathematics-infused curriculum reported that the subject was more important and interesting than did the students in the comparison group (controlling for responses on the presurvey). There were no significant differences between the groups on relevance. However, changes between the presurvey and postsurvey data revealed a decrease in reports from students in the infusion curriculum about the relevance of mathematics to their lives (Burghardt et al. 2010).

An unpublished study of a school-based engineering project for 6th and 7th graders similarly showed positive effects on students' attitudes. The study included a comparison group of students who did not participate in the project, and students were surveyed both before and after the project. Students who participated in the project (designing a prosthetic arm) reported increased interest in engineering as a potential career as well as increased confidence in mathematics and science, although girls scored lower than boys in terms of their interest in engineering as a career and in their beliefs that they could become engineers (High et al. 2010).

Turning to out-of-school programs, in an unpublished evaluation of the Techbridge program, 367 girls (44 percent of the total number of girls) who had participated in the program from 2000 to 2007 completed surveys. Nearly 90 percent of the respondents reported that Techbridge had increased their interest in STEM; asked to identify what got them most interested in STEM, 72 percent cited hands-on projects and 16 percent said it was field trips (Ancheta 2008).

Evaluation of another enrichment program for high school youth, integrating engineering with biology concepts in a health care context using lecture and hands-on activities, also revealed positive effects on interest. On post-program surveys 50 percent of participants reported increased interest and more positive attitudes toward science and engineering (Monterastelli et al. 2011).

In a study of an all-girl summer camp with a STEM focus, the girls' self-report of the likelihood of their pursuing a career in mathematics, science, or engineering rose from an average of 6.3 to 7.4 on a 10-point scale (Plotowski et al. 2008).

The results of other studies have been less clear. An unpublished evaluation of Project Exploration in Chicago, an out-of-school program for middle school–aged girls and minority students, summarized findings from surveys and interviews of participants during and after their participation. The responses showed greater interest and confidence in science, but these were not assessed at the beginning of the program and no control group was used (Chi and Snow 2010).

Four studies of robotics programs showed somewhat mixed results. A published study of a 4-H robotics program revealed no significant differences in attitude between program participants and a control group of nonparticipants (Baker et al. 2008). But in an unpublished evaluation of FIRST robotics, an out-of-school program where students work in teams to design and build robots, students' self-report on retrospective surveys (57 percent response rate) indicated higher interest in science and technology (89 percent of respondents) and in science and technology careers (69 percent of respondents) (Melchoir et al. 2005). In an evaluation of an out-of-school program that engages students in computer programming and engineering using robotic kits, 76 percent of students showed an improvement in their attitudes toward science and technology on pre and post surveys (Martin et al. 2011). Finally, in an evaluation of a robotics and geospatial program, about half of students reported more positive attitudes at the end of the program (Nugent et al. 2010).

Identity

Few of the studies considered by the committee examined identity. A commissioned paper on the topic reported that only three were conducted in the context of integrated STEM programs, and they were qualitative case studies.

The first study examined identity development in the context of science clubs for low-income middle school youth to pursue projects of their own choosing (Rahm 2008). The study showed that youth who were successful in the science clubs took on positions and roles that integrated their own histories and cultural backgrounds with science and that these roles were recognized by individuals who were more knowledgeable, such as the teachers running the clubs. The researcher posited that the formally acknowledged hybrid roles allowed the youth to try out ideas and ways of being that may have previously seemed out of reach or culturally incongruent (i.e., inconsistent with the culture of the students' families or communities). She further suggested that the flexibility of the program, the value of doing a project both in and for the community, or the openness that allowed the students to define their own projects may all have been important elements in supporting development of a STEM-related identity (Rahm 2008).

A similar argument is made by Calabrese Barton and Tan (2010a) in the context of a technology-rich integrated science and engineering program focused on green energy. The researchers argue that as the youth in the program appropriated tools and resources through the program in ways that were culturally congruent, they developed roles as "community science experts"—they were seen as experts on matters in the community and in science, able to bring the two together. The study report describes the process by which the youth chose to investigate the urban heat island effect in their city and how they designed their study through scientific, engineering, and place-based concerns. They then wove these concerns together in a series of digital narratives to educate their community about their findings. Their role as experts was recognized and legitimized by teachers, scientists, and community members, and this acknowledgment was essential in supporting both their identity development and their learning (Calabrese Barton and Tan 2010a).

In a follow-up study, Calabrese Barton and Tan (2010b) analyzed the participants' narratives describing their involvement in the green energy project over multiple years. These narratives revealed how the youths' identities as community science experts and activists were carried from project to project and into new communities through public service announcements, scientific documentaries, and a new green roof for the building where the club was held, which the youth described as visible reminders of their hard work, what they know, and whom they influenced.

The findings from these three studies suggest that identity development may be supported by integrated experiences because such experiences support a range of ways of knowing, employ project- or problem-based approaches that allow youth to follow their interests, and can focus on problems relevant in local communities.

Summary

The findings about whether integrated STEM supports interest and continuation in STEM are mixed; there are promising indications, but the studies vary in quality. The measures of interest are typically not very sophisticated and do not take into account different phases of interest development. Also, many studies use before/after designs without any comparison groups. This is not a very powerful design for determining causal effects, so results are difficult to interpret.

Research on identity is at a very preliminary stage. The studies reviewed were qualitative and involved a very limited number of participants, but seem to indicate that open-endedness and links to students' culture and community are important, as is the opportunity for students to be recognized as experts.

For both types of research, larger-scale studies and studies that incorporate a wider range of methods are needed.

CONCLUSIONS

Research on integrated STEM experiences suggests that they may be promising for supporting both learning in and across the STEM disciplines and the development of STEM-related interest and identity. The research base is limited, however, in terms of the design of the studies, the populations of students involved in them, the outcome measures used, and the extent to which research examines the mechanisms underlying learning in integrated STEM contexts.

In terms of learning and achievement, for integrated STEM education to be successful students need to be able to move back and forth between the acquisition of disciplinary knowledge and skill and their application to problems that call on competencies from multiple disciplines. Students need to be competent with discipline-specific representations and be able to translate between discipline-specific representations thereby exhibiting what some scholars refer to as "representational fluency." Participation in shared practices, such as modeling in engineering, science, and mathematics, may support such fluency.

Integrated STEM experiences do appear to provide opportunities for students to productively engage in ways that can transform their identity with respect to STEM, and this effect may be particularly strong for populations that have historically struggled in STEM classes and are underrepresented in STEM higher education programs and professions.

The committee's review of the research illuminated specific areas where further research is needed. For example, there is a need for more studies that measure or document students' ability to make connections across disciplines or to demonstrate representational fluency. Few studies focus on the development of interest and identity in formal educational settings, and even fewer address their development in the context of integrated STEM, in either formal or informal settings. Finally, although there is a body of research showing how integrated STEM experiences can be designed to foster connections between science and mathematics, there is a clear need to extend this research to more grade levels and to show more connections with engineering and technology.

More generally, the evidence base needs to be both deepened and broadened to support strong conclusions about the effectiveness of integrated STEM and an understanding of underlying mechanisms. Weaknesses in the research that need to be addressed include impoverished descriptions of interventions, lack of common terms and theories, and the need to use a wider range of methods with a better match of the questions to the designs. Current measures and descriptions of integration, as both a pedagogical method and a student outcome, lack reliability and validity.

All of these research-related issues are explored in greater depth in Chapter 6.

REFERENCES

Ancheta, R. 2008. 2008 qualitative and quantitative longitudinal evaluation of Techbridge.

Barker, B.S., G. Nugent, N. Grandgenett, and A. Hampton. 2008 (Spring). Examining 4-H robotics in the learning of science, engineering, and technology topics and the related student attitudes. Journal of Youth Development: Bridging Research and Practice 2(3). Article 0803FA001.

Baumgartner, E., and B.J. Reiser. 1997. Inquiry through design: Situating and supporting inquiry through design projects in high school science classrooms. Annual Meeting of the National Association for Research in Science Teaching, Oak Brook, Illinois.

Berlin, D.F., and H. Lee. 2005. Integrating science and mathematics education: Historical analysis. School Science and Mathematics 105(1):15–24.

Berlin, D.F., and H. Lee. 2003. A bibliography of integrated science and mathematics teaching and learning literature, Vol. 2: 1991–2001. School Science and Mathematics Association Topics for Teachers Series Number 7. Columbus, OH: ERIC Clearinghouse for Science, Mathematics, and Environmental Education.

Bozick, R., and B. Dalton. 2013. Balancing career and technical education with academic coursework: The consequences for mathematics achievement in high school. Educational Evaluation and Policy Analysis 35(2):123–138.

Brown, B. 2004. Discursive identity: Assimilation into the culture of science and its implications for minority students. Journal of Research in Scence Teaching 41(8):810–834.

Brown, B. 2006. "It isn't no slang that can be said about this stuff": Language, identity, and apropriating science discourse. Journal of Research in Scence Teaching 43(1):96–126.

Burghardt, M.D., D. Hecht, M. Russo, J. Lauckhardt, and M. Hacker. 2010. A study of mathematics infusion in middle school technology education classes. Journal of Technology Education 22(1):58–74.

Calabrese Barton, A., and E. Tan. 2010a. We be burnin': Agency, identity and learning in a green energy program. Journal of the Learning Sciences 19(2):187–229.

Calabrese Barton, A., and E. Tan. 2010b. The new green roof: Activism, science and greening the community. Journal of Canadian Journal of Science, Mathematics and Technology Education 10(3): 207–222.

Calabrese Barton, A., H. Kang, E. Tan, T. O'Neill, and C. Brecklin. 2012. Crafting a future in science: Tracing middle school girls' identity work over time and space. American Education Research Journal 50(1):37–75.

Carlone, H.B., J. Haun-Frank, and A. Webb. 2011. Assessing equity beyond knowledge- and skills based outcomes: A comparative ethnography of two fourth-grade reform-based science classrooms. Journal of Research in Science Teaching 48(5):459–485.

Chi, B., and J.Z. Snow. 2010. Project Exploration (PE): 10-year retrospective program evaluation summative report, submitted to the Noyce Foundation. Available at www.projectexploration.org/about-us/publications/10 years (retrieved January 21, 2014).

Crismond, D. 2001. Learning and using science ideas when doing investigate-and-redesign tasks: A study of naïve, novice and expert designers doing constrained and scaffolded design work. Journal of Research in Science Teaching 38(7):791–820. doi:10.1002/tea.1032.

Crismond, D., and R. Adams. 2012. The informed design teaching and learning matrix. Journal of Engineering Education 101(4):738–797.

Czerniak, C.M., W.B. Weber, A. Sandmann, and J. Ahern. 1999. A literature review of science and mathematics integration. School Science and Mathematics 99(8):421–430.

Dickes, A.C., and P. Sengupta. 2012. Learning natural selection in 4th grade with multi-agent-based computational models. Research in Science Education 43(3):921–953.

DiSessa, A. 2000. Changing minds. Cambridge, MA: MIT Press.

Fortus, D., R.C. Dershimer, J. Krajcik, R.W. Marx, and R. Mamlok-Naaman. 2005. Design-based science and real-world problem-solving. International Journal of Science Education 27(7):855–879.

Fortus, D., R.C. Dershimer, J. Krajcik, R.W. Marx, and R. Mamlok-Naaman. 2004. Design based science and student learning. Journal of Research in Science Teaching 41(10):1081.

Hartzler, D.S. 2000. A meta-analysis of studies conducted on integrated curriculum programs and their effects on student achievement. Ed.D. Dissertation, Indiana University, Bloomington.

Hedges, L.V., J.A. Shymansky, and G. Woodworth. 1989. A practical guide to modern methods of meta-analysis. Washington: National Science Teachers Association.

Hidi, S., and M. Ainley. 2008. Interest and self-regulation: Relationships between two variables that influence learning. In D. H. Schunk and B. J. Zimmerman (Eds.), Motivation and self-regulated learning: Theory, research, and application (pp. 77–109). Mahwah, NJ: Erlbaum.

Hidi, S., and K.A. Renninger. 2006. The four-phase model of interest development. Educational Psychologist 41(2):111–127.

High, K., J. Thomas, and A. Redmond. August, 2010. Expanding middle school science and math learning: Measuring the effect of multiple engineering projects. Paper presented at the P-12 Engineering and Design Education Research Summit, Seaside, OR.

Hmelo-Silver, C.E., S. Marathe, and L. Liu. 2007. Fish swim, rocks sit, lungs breathe: Expert-novice understanding of complex systems. Journal of the Learning Sciences 16(3):307–331. doi: 10.1080/10508400701413401.

Holland, D., W. Lachicotte Jr., D. Skinner, and C. Cain. 2001. Identity and agency in cultural worlds. Cambridge, MA: Harvard University Press.

Hurley, M.M. 2001. Reviewing integrated science and mathematics: The search for evidence and definitions from new perspectives. School Science and Mathematics 101(5):259–268.

Kolodner, J.L. 2002. Facilitating the learning of design practices: Lessons learned from an inquiry into science education. Available at http://scholar.lib.vt.edu/ejournals/JITE/v39n3/kolodner.html. (retrieved August 1, 2013).

Kozma, R. 2003. The material features of multiple representations and their cognitive and social affordances for science understanding. Learning and Instruction 13:205–226.

Krapp, A. 2007. An educational–psychological conceptualization of interest. International Journal of Educational and Vocational Guidance 7:5–21.

Lehrer, R., and L. Schauble. 2000. Modeling in mathematics and science. In R. Glaser (Ed.), Advances in instructional psychology (Vol. 5, pp. 101–159). Mahwah, NJ: Lawrence Erlbaum Associates.

Lehrer, R., and L. Schauble. 2006. Scientific thinking and science literacy: Supporting development in learning in contexts. In W. Damon, R. M. Lerner, K. A. Renninger and I. E. Sigel (Eds.), Handbook of child psychology, 6th ed. (Vol. 4). Hoboken, NJ: John Wiley and Sons.

Lehrer, R., L. Schauble, and D. Lucas. 2008. Supporting development of the epistemology of inquiry. Cognitive Development 24:512–529.

Martin, F.G., M. Scribner-MacLean, S. Christy, I. Rudnicki, R. Londhe, C. Manning, and I.F. Goodman. 2011. Reflections on iCODE: Using web technology and hands-on projects to engage urban youth in computer science and engineering. Auton Robot 30:265–280.

Mehalik, M., Y. Doppelt, and C.D. Schunn. 2005. Addressing performance and equity of a design-based, systems approach for teaching science in eighth grade. Annual Meeting of the American Educational Research Association, Montreal.

Mehalik, M.M., Y. Doppelt, and C.D. Schunn. 2008. Middle-school science through design based learning versus scripted inquiry: Better overall science concept learning and equity gap reduction. Journal of Engineering Education 97(1):71–85.

Melchoir, A., F. Cohen, T. Cutter, and T. Leavitt. 2005. More than robots: An evaluation of the FIRST Robotics competition: Participant and institutional impacts. Available at http://dev1.raiderrobotix.org/wp-content/uploads/2012/08/FRC_eval_finalrpt.pdf (retrieved January 14, 2014).

Monterastelli, T., T. Bayles, and J. Ross. 2011. High school outreach program: Attracting young ladies with "engineering in health care." Proceedings of the American Society for Engineering Education, 2011 Annual Conference and Exposition, Vancouver.

NAE (National Academy of Engineering) and NRC (National Research Council). 2009. Engineering in K-12 education: Understanding the status and improving the prospects. L. Katehi, G. Pearson, and M. Feder (Eds.). Committee on K–12 Engineering Education. Washington: National Academies Press.

NCTL (National Center for Technological Literacy). 2005. Engineering the Future: Designing the World of the 21st Century. Boston, MA: Museum of Science.

Nathan, M.J., R. Srisurichan, C. Walkington, M. Wolfgram, C. Williams, and M.W. Alibali. 2013. Cohesion as a mechanism of STEM integration. Journal of Engineering Education. (Special issue on representation in engineering education.)

Nugent, G., B. Barker, N. Grandgennett, and V. Adamchuk. 2010. Impact of robotics and geospatial technology interventions on youth STEM learning and attitudes. Journal of Research in Technology Education 42(4):391–408.

Pang, J., and R. Good. 2000. A review of the integration of science and mathematics: Implications for further research. School Science and Mathematics 100(2):73–82.

Penner, D.E., N.D. Giles, R. Lehrer, and L. Schauble. 1997. Building functional models: Designing an elbow. Journal of Research in Science Teaching 34(2):1–20.

Penner, D.E., R. Lehrer, and L. Schauble. 1998. From physical models to biomechanics: A design-based modeling approach. Journal of the Learning Sciences 7:429–449.

Petrosino, A.J., V. Svihla, and S. Brophy. 2008. Engineering skills for understanding and improving K–12 engineering education in the United States. Presented at the National Academy of Engineering/National Research Council workshop on K–12 Engineering Education. Washington, DC.

Plotowski, P., M.A. Sheline, M. Dill, and J. Noble. 2008. Empowering girls: Measuring the impact of science technology and engineering preview summer camps (STEPS). Proceedings, American Society for Engineering Education. 2008 Annual Conference and Exposition, Pittsburgh.

Rahm, J. 2008. Urban youths' hybrid identity projects in science practices at the margin: A look inside a school-museum-scientist partnership project and an afterschool science program. Cultural Studies of Science Education 3(1):97–121.

Renninger, K.A. 2009. Interest and identity development in instruction: An inductive model. Educational Psychologist 44(2):1–14.

Renninger, K.A. 2010. Working with and cultivating interest, self-efficacy, and self-regulation. In D. Preiss and R. Sternberg (Eds.), Innovations in educational psychology: Perspectives on learning, teaching and human development (pp. 107–138). New York: Springer.

Renninger, K.A., and S. Hidi. 2011. Revisiting the conceptualization, measurement, and generation of interest. Educational Psychologist 46(3):168–184.

Sadler, P.M., H.P. Coyle, and M. Schwartz. 2000. Engineering competitions in the middle school classroom: Key elements in developing effective design challenges. Journal of the Learning Sciences 9(3):299–327. doi:10.11207/S15327809JLS0903_3.

Sansone, C. 2009. What's interest got to do with it?: Potential trade-offs in the self-regulation of motivation. In J. P. Forgas, R. Baumeister, and D. Tice (Eds.), Psychology of self-regulation: Cognitive, affective, and motivational processes (pp. 35–51). New York: Psychology Press.

Schauble, L., R. Glaser, R.A. Duschl, S. Schulze, and J. John. 1995. Students' understanding of the objectives and procedures of experimentation in the science classroom. Journal of the Learning Sciences 4(2):131–166.

Sengupta, P., and U. Wilensky. 2011. Lowering the learning threshold: Multi-agent-based models and learning electricity. In M.S. Khine and M. Saleh (Eds.). Models and modeling in science education (pp. 141–171). Netherlands: Springer.

Sherin, B. 2001. How students understand physics equations. Cognition and Instruction 1:479–541.

Stone, J.R., C. Alfeld, and D. Pearson. 2008. Rigor and relevance: Enhancing high school students' math skills through career and technical education. American Educational Research Journal 45(3):767–795.

Tran, N.A., and M.J. Nathan. 2010a. An investigation of the relationship between pre-college engineering studies and student achievement in science and mathematics. Journal of Engineering Education 99(2):143–157.

Tran, N., and M.J. Nathan. 2010b. Effects of pre-college engineering studies on mathematics and science achievements for high school students. International Journal of Engineering Education 26(5):1049–1060. (Special issue on applications of engineering education research.)

Wilensky, U. 2003. Statistical mechanics for secondary school: The GasLab modeling toolkit. International Journal of Computers for Mathematical Learning 8(1):1–41.

Wilensky, U., and K. Reisman. 2006. Thinking like a wolf, a sheep, or a firefly: Learning biology through constructing and testing computational theories—an embodied modeling approach. Cognition and Instruction 24(2):171–209.

Wortham, S. 2006. Learning identity: The joint emergence of social identification and academic learning. New York: Cambridge University Press.

4

Implications of the Research for Designing Integrated STEM Experiences

The recent surge of interest in designing programs that successfully engage students in integrated STEM learning experiences has created a demand for guidance about what constitutes "effective" integrated STEM education. Yet, as evidenced in the previous chapter, research on integrated STEM is at the preliminary stages and there are few large-scale studies that systematically compare different approaches to integration. However, the smaller-scale research efforts in the field can be supplemented with relevant findings from research on cognition, learning, and teaching to formulate hypotheses about how to design effective integrated STEM learning experiences and the limitations that need to be considered.

In this chapter we identify implications for design based on the research reviewed in the previous chapter, as well as evidence related to cognition and learning more generally. In the first section, we explore research on how people learn in order to determine how integrated experiences in STEM might support learning, thinking, interest, and identity development, and, conversely, why they might do little to change students' attitudes, thinking, and behaviors.

Drawing on these discussions together with the research findings and limitations reviewed in Chapter 3, we identify issues related to designing integrated STEM experiences so that they more effectively support learning within and across the STEM disciplines. We also lay out important areas for future research and development.

INTEGRATED EXPERIENCES AND HOW PEOPLE LEARN[1]

In this section we draw on a substantial body of research on cognition and learning to explore the mechanisms by which integration might support, or be an obstacle to, learning within and across the STEM disciplines. Several decades of research in cognitive psychology, the learning sciences, educational psychology, curriculum and instruction, and other fields have shed light on how the mind works and how best to support learning. This research provides a foundation for understanding how and why integrated STEM experiences can support improvement in learning and thinking, where they might pose difficulties for learners, and how they can be designed to be more effective.

The committee considered findings from studies on learning and teaching across a range of research traditions including those informed by situative, sociocultural, cognitive, pragmatist, and constructivist theoretical perspectives. Findings obtained using diverse research methods, applied across several fields and perspectives, converge to create a picture of learning as an active process that is deeply social, embedded in a particular cultural context, and enhanced by intentional support provided by more knowledgeable individuals, be they peers, mentors, or teachers.

Based on what is known about cognition and learning, it is possible to hypothesize both advantages and disadvantages for learning from integrated experiences. But such experiences have only recently become a focus of research in STEM educational contexts, so important research questions remain. These are discussed in the final chapter of this report.

We begin with a discussion of key basic processes of cognition and learning and their implications for integrated instruction—how it supports learning and where it might introduce challenges. It appears that integration can be effective because basic qualities of cognition favor connected concepts over unconnected concepts; the former are better organized for future retrieval and meaning making than the latter. But it can also impede learning because it (1) places excessive demands on resource-limited cognitive processes such as attention and working memory, or (2) attempts to make bridges between ideas that were not well learned, or (3) obscures important differences in STEM disciplines about how knowledge is constructed and revised.

---

[1]This section is based on the review of the cognitive sciences literature conducted by Eli M. Silk and Christian D. Schunn, University of Pittsburgh, and on commissioned papers by Mary Gauvain, University of California, Riverside, Angela Calabrese Barton, Michigan State University, and Steven Marc Weisberg, Temple University.

Given the focus of this report and the breadth of the research on cognition and learning, it is impossible to provide a detailed review of all the current research (for a summary see NRC 2000). Instead, we focus on the aspects of cognition and learning that, in the committee's judgment, are relevant to an understanding of integrated STEM.

Building Connected Knowledge Structures

A major insight from research on cognition and learning is that the organization of knowledge—that is, the ability to make connections between concepts and representations[2]—is key to the development of expertise in a domain. Multiple studies have shown that experts do not just know more about a domain, they understand how ideas are related to each other and their relative importance and usefulness in the domain. They also notice features and meaningful patterns of information in the context of their field of expertise that are often not noticed by novices (see NRC 2000, Chapter 2, for a summary of research on expert knowledge). This organized knowledge gives experts multiple advantages for thinking and learning. For example, when they approach a new problem they are able to attend to its deep, structural aspects rather than surface features (Chi et al. 1981) and thus connect new tasks or concepts to prior experiences more readily and more meaningfully.

The importance of organized knowledge relates directly to some of the aims of STEM integration described in Chapter 3, such as helping students connect ideas learned at different stages of project-based learning or developing students' representational fluency. Thus one way to frame the goals of learning is to think of it as helping novices build and reorganize their knowledge to develop more expertlike competence in a domain. For integrated STEM it is important to determine how to help students both build knowledge in individual disciplines and learn to make connections among them.

The foundation of knowledge building and rebuilding is the learner's experience. All new knowledge builds on existing knowledge and involves making connections from previous experiences to the current context (NRC 2000, 2007). But learners often do not spontaneously relate the knowledge they possess, however relevant, to new tasks, a phenomenon referred to as a problem of transfer (see the discussion of transfer below as well as NRC

---

[2] A representation expresses or symbolizes an idea or relationship. Examples of representations include drawings, schematics, graphs, and mathematical equations.

2000, Chapter 3); they often need cues or explicit supports to help them make connections.

One emerging view (e.g., Koedinger et al. 2012; Rau et al. 2012) is that integrated approaches benefit individuals who already have knowledge pertinent to the integrating elements, whereas individuals with limited knowledge are less adept at building connections among conceptual structures. This situation can produce so-called aptitude-treatment interactions; that is, an intervention produces different results depending on an individual's initial level of knowledge or skill (e.g., Cronbach and Snow 1977; Serlin and Levin 1980).

Integrated STEM experiences vary depending on whether they are designed to target discipline-specific knowledge and skills or to support integration of knowledge across disciplines. In some cases a context or activity incorporates knowledge, and requires use of practices from more than one discipline, but students are expected to demonstrate learning gains in only one discipline. In other cases, experiences are designed to help students advance in more than one discipline, but students are not expected to demonstrate an ability to make connections across disciplines. And a smaller number of integrated experiences are designed to help students make and demonstrate connections between ideas across disciplines.

Depending on the outcomes of interest, an integrated learning experience should take account of students' knowledge within individual disciplines as well as help them make connections between disciplines, drawing on the disciplinary knowledge they already possess.

Transfer

Transfer is one of the principal goals of learning in school: students should be able to take the knowledge and skills learned in one context and apply them in another. Typically, teaching for transfer aims to increase transfer within a discipline. Integrated STEM educational experiences, by design, ask students to engage in the transfer of disciplinary knowledge and, ideally, enable the students to reliably transfer their knowledge to other areas and activities in the future.

Transfer can be explored at a variety of levels—from one context to another, one set of concepts to another, one school subject to another, one year of school to another, across school, and to everyday nonschool activities. A recent NRC report on transfer in the context of learning 21st century skills (NRC 2012) found that there is little research on how to help learners transfer competencies learned in one discipline or topic area to another. The report identifies features of instruction that may support transfer (NRC 2012, p. 9):

- Using multiple and varied representations of concepts and tasks
- Encouraging elaboration, questioning, and explanation
- Engaging learners in challenging tasks
- Teaching with examples and cases
- Priming student motivation
- Using formative assessment

Many of these features are present in integrated STEM programs, but research is needed to assess whether and how they support development of both disciplinary competence and the ability to make connections across disciplines.

Integrating Across Multiple Representations

Representations that express or symbolize an idea or relationship are an important element of disciplinary knowledge and can facilitate learning. In STEM disciplines, each form of representation highlights or amplifies an aspect of a natural or designed system while simultaneously reducing or summarizing its essence (Latour 1999). Within a discipline, the development of connections among different representations is an important way in which disciplinary knowledge grows (Latour 1999, p. 24). Kozma and colleagues (2000) reported on integrative thinking among chemists who made explicit and implicit connections between a structural drawing, an experimental design, and data and used language to support these connections. Consequently, the chemists were able to reason with one representation (a drawing), while making inferences about another (e.g., a spectrum).

In integrated STEM learning experiences, students often need to make connections across different kinds of representations from a single discipline and learn to recognize how representations from different disciplines are related. For example, high school geometry students who use interactive software such as the Geometer's Sketchpad® may construct multiple cases for exploring invariant relations that exist when a triangle is inscribed in a circle. The initial representations will start out as visual-spatial, but the students may be called on to present verbal proof in support of their conjectures (Nathan et al. 2013), thus demonstrating connections between visual and verbal representations in a single discipline. Similarly, students participating in an engineering project on ballistic behavior may use geometry modeling software, such as AutoDesk, to formalize a sketch into the design of a device such as a catapult. They will make connections across disciplinary boundaries when they relate the specifications of the device created in the CAD/CAM system (technology) to trigonometric relations (geometry) used in the quadratic equations (algebra) that model the kinematic laws (physics) that specify the ideal trajectory of the ballistic flight.

Psychological research has shown important benefits for learning and performance in people who make connections between multiple representations of a particular concept or relationship. Evidence from both behavioral (e.g., Griffin et al. 1994; Stenning and Oberlander 1995) and neuroscience research (e.g., Dehaene et al. 1999) points to a dual system of linguistic and spatial representations that supports mathematical reasoning. Tabachneck (1992; Tabachneck et al. 1994) showed that an expert in economics successfully conveyed an economic situation that was thought to be out of reach for novices by combining graphical and verbal representations. Schwartz (1995) found that the availability of multiple representations played a key role in students' generation of abstract representations. And Case and Okamoto (1996) demonstrated that when children form an integrated conceptual understanding, they exhibit new capabilities. For example, they can understand a concept presented in one modality using their understanding of another system that shares deep conceptual structure but has vastly different surface features and operations. Each of these cases represents discipline-specific integrative thinking.

Learning from Real-World Situations

One hallmark of integrated approaches, though not unique to them, is the use of real-world situations or problems. They can bring STEM fields alive for students and deepen their learning, but they may also pose particular challenges for them.

There is evidence that use of detailed concrete situations with rich perceptual information can prevent students from identifying the abstract structural characteristics needed to transfer their experiences to other settings. Goldstone and Sakamoto (2003) and Sloutsky and colleagues (Kaminski et al.

2005, 2006a, 2006b; Sloutsky et al. 2005) found disadvantages to increasing levels of perceptual richness, especially when the added features were irrelevant to the structural features the students were meant to learn. Goldstone and Sakamoto (2003) found that the effects of the perceptual richness differed depending on students' initial capabilities: students who were already able to attend to the abstract features of a situation were unlikely to be distracted by perceptual richness, whereas those who had difficulty grasping the abstract information were more likely to be distracted by superficial features.

It may be that real-world situations can be designed to encourage students to attend to the critical (as opposed to irrelevant) features of the situation. Kaminski and colleagues (2009) tested this idea by having students learn a mathematical rule either with entirely generic materials, so the rule's connection to the symbols was entirely arbitrary, or with materials in a familiar context that follows the rule (in this case pictures of beakers of liquid combined with some left over). They found again that the relevant concreteness had advantages for learning of the particular rule, but that the generic materials resulted in better transfer to another context that followed the same rule but in which the objects didn't compel the rule as they had in the relevant concrete learning materials. Although Kaminski and colleagues do not test claims about rich contexts directly (their "concrete" condition is an abstract image meant to resemble real objects), this work does reveal some of the trade-offs for perceptually rich and lean curriculum materials when measuring learning and transfer.

One implication of this research is that classroom instruction designed to promote the use of knowledge across different contexts should include instruction in the abstract or generic representations of the concept being taught. Teachers should not expect students to be able to infer the underlying symbolic or abstract representation of a problem by solving the problem using a single concrete instantiation (e.g., Goldstone and Sakamoto 2003; Goldstone and Son 2005; Kaminski et al. 2006a, 2006b; Sloutsky et al. 2005).

Cognitive Limitations: Attention and Memory

Research in cognitive psychology demonstrates that the amount of information a learner can simultaneously attend to and process deeply is very limited (Anderson 1996, 2004; Miller 1956). One's intellectual abilities can appear to be outsized, however, when one effortlessly perceives information as connected and meaningful. Strings of random numbers will quickly exceed an individual's information processing capabilities, unless s/he can readily group them in familiar "chunks," such as important dates or the time (in minutes and seconds) needed to run a race of a certain distance (Ericsson et al. 1980).

When presented with multiple sources of information, learners must direct their attention to each individual source, encode separate pieces of information, manage the stored information, and discern the relevant connections. Split attention—simultaneously dividing one's attention between competing sources of information—is cognitively demanding and can be a major obstacle to understanding and learning. The split-attention effect is evidenced by difficulties in storing and processing information that is physically separated (Mayer 2001; Mayer and Moreno 1998; Sweller et al. 1998). But it can be remedied: student learning improves when individual sources of information are visually integrated so they can be processed together in a single image (Bobis et al. 1993; Chandler and Sweller 1992, 1996; Mayer and Anderson 1991, 1992; Moreno and Mayer 1999; Mwangi and Sweller 1998; Sweller et al. 1990).

These aspects of cognition point to a potential drawback of integration: without effective guidance, the effort to make connections among multiple disciplines in the context of a complex problem or situation could overwhelm students and inhibit learning. Design of integrated experiences must balance the richness of integration and real-world contexts against the constraints of the cognitive demands of processing information that is separated in time, in space, or across disciplines and types of representation.

Learning by Doing and Embodied Cognition

Integrated STEM experiences typically call on students to engage in activities that involve the use of tools or manipulation of objects, and claims have been made that this use enhances learning. Although such instructional strategies are widely used in mathematics education (e.g., Fuson et al. 2000; Clements 2000) and mathematics education research (Chao et al. 2000; Martin and Schwartz 2005; Uttal et al. 1997), there is little research in other STEM fields on the relationship between physical manipulation of objects and learning, although some studies of physics learning do demonstrate benefits. One study reported that students who actually felt the angular momentum change when a rotating bicycle wheel was held performed better on written tests about angular momentum than students who merely watched other students hold the bicycle wheel (Kontra et al. 2012).

A related approach to understanding learning involves embodied cognition, the perspective that cognition occurs in a physical organism interacting with its environment; to understand the structures that mediate learning, one must consider the brain, body, and environment as an interactive unit. This approach considers forms of "embodied learning" such as gesture, sketching, and arranging objects, which can help mitigate the brain's limited processing ability (Kirsh and Maglio 1994).

Embodied experiences may provide pathways for coordinating mathematical and scientific concepts. For example, children in elementary grades

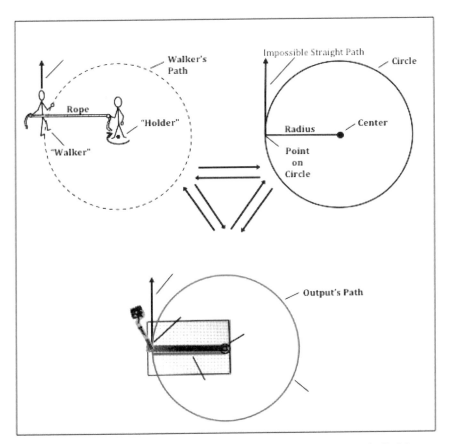

FIGURE 4-1 Three complementary representations of rotary motion: embodied (upper left), geometrical (upper right), and mechanical/linkage (lower). SOURCE: Bolger et al. (2010). Reprinted with permission.

are often expected to understand how simple machines work. But developing mechanistic reasoning is challenging, and many elementary students fail to anticipate or explain how interactions among components of the devices account for how they work (Bolger et al. 2012; Metz 1985).

Simple forms of embodiment and mathematical representation appear to substantially support the development of mechanistic reasoning. For example, in one study, children participated in rope walks, in which one student, "the holder," acted as a fixed pivot (the fulcrum) and the other, "the walker" at the other end of the rope, as the end of a lever arm (Figure 4-1). When the child at the end of the rope attempted to walk in a direction perpendicular to the line joining the two children, the path was constrained to be circular. Challenged to represent the essential difference between ends of lever arms near and far from the fulcrum, by walking toward and away from the holder students came to see the usefulness of circles and their properties for describing how linkages (connected levers) function (Bolger et al. 2010, 2011).

Social Aspects of Learning and Cognition

Social and cultural factors are fundamental to all learning experiences and particularly important in integrated experiences, which typically require students to work with each other and actively engage in discussion, joint decision making, and collaborative problem solving. Integrated STEM education often involves extensive collaboration among teachers and students, and therefore its success depends on the design and effectiveness of the social aspects of the approach.

Social supports for learning are ubiquitous, occur in a variety of settings, and are present in all cultures (Lancy et al. 2009). Key ingredients for effective learning are the availability of appropriate support to help learners engage in an activity in a meaningful way, the gradual withdrawal of these supports as the learner's competence increases, and instruction and guidance in the use of tools that support learning (NRC 2000).

Social processes of learning are inherent to three major components of integrated STEM education: the participation of the learners, the assistance provided by the teacher(s), and the nature and meaning of the learning activity itself. Because research has shown that not all forms of social experience are conducive to learning (Slavin 1983), careful attention to the design of social processes in integrated STEM education is essential.

The social contexts that support learning include the physical settings themselves and the social psychological processes that occur in these settings. Learning is promoted by many social processes—observation, imitation, regulation of joint attention, demonstration, instruction, and shaping. Research has shown, for example, that children learn how to solve problems, including how to attend to important features and the knowledge and strategies needed to solve problems, by observing more experienced partners solve similar problems. Research has also demonstrated that learning can result when social support is carefully arranged, learning is monitored, and adjustments are made if learning strays too far from the goal (Gauvain 2001).

What children learn from observation and collaborative activity depends on their developmental status. Whereas preschool children benefit from assistance in understanding problems, following rules, and manipulating materials, school-age children gain more from help with strategies. Research suggests that the social psychological processes available in the learning environment, including the composition and activities of learning groups and the involvement of the teacher, are important design features for integrated STEM education. Social guidance and support for learning also exist in cultural tools that aid thinking and problem solving and in the type and structure of the learning activities in which children engage.

Certain social processes that support learning involve deliberate efforts to convey knowledge and strategies. Among these are instruction in the zone of proximal development (Vygotsky 1978), scaffolding (Wood and Middleton 1978), and peer collaboration.

The zone of proximal development (ZPD) is defined as "the distance between the actual developmental level as determined by independent problem solving and the level of potential development as determined through problem solving under adult guidance or in collaboration with more capable peers" (Vygotsky 1978, p. 86). The ZPD is the region of sensitivity for learning in a particular domain.

One of the primary means by which teachers and other more experienced partners (such as more advanced peers, older students or parents) support children's learning in the ZPD is with a learner-focused instructional technique known as scaffolding, which involves verbal and nonverbal efforts tailored to the learner's needs to help him or her engage with a challenging activity (Renninger and Granott 2005; Wood et al. 1976, 1978; Wood and Middleton 1975). For instance, an activity, such as planning errands, may be broken into a series of actions (Gauvain and Rogoff 1989) and strategies for solving the problem (how to do the errands in an efficient manner) modeled by the more experienced partner, who meanwhile encourages and supports the learner's involvement. The more experienced partner may also take on the more difficult parts of the problem so the learner can concentrate on easier parts that are less taxing to attention and memory (Gauvain 1992).

At both the elementary and secondary school levels children's understanding and skills can be improved when peers work together on challenging tasks, especially when the exchanges are cooperative (Gauvain 2001; Light and Littleton 1999). Peer interaction can be more open and egalitarian than interaction with adults (Piaget 1952) and therefore can generate unique learning opportunities. Peer interactions such as tutoring, discussion, or joint problem solving offer different opportunities for learning because peers can define and structure a problem in a way that is mutually accessible (Ellis and Gauvain 1992). Peer interaction can also make different points of view available to learners, and they can take these perspectives into account in their reasoning.

Research has focused on collaborative problem solving by peers in the classroom in several disciplines, including mathematics and science (Light and Littleton 1999). Findings confirm that learning emerges from the joint construction of understanding through social processes such as discussion, argumentation, and negotiation. Even when classroom situations are not set up as collaborations, children often seek support for learning from peers, which can aid learning (Karabenick and Newman 2006).

Summary

Integrated approaches to STEM education are generally consistent with what is known about effective ways to support learning. They can promote the development of rich, conceptual knowledge in a particular discipline and provide contexts for students to build competence in problem solving and develop skills that apply across disciplines. The use of physical objects in the course of project-based learning may facilitate intellectual performance and learning, because it can help make up for the limitations of the brain's processing capacity. Furthermore, because working with physical objects typically fosters interaction between students and requires communication and collaboration, it can leverage the social aspects of learning in ways that traditional approaches to instruction often do not.

At the same time, integrated instruction can pose challenges to learning and must be carefully designed with these challenges mind. One challenge is posed by the use of real-world contexts that are complex and characterized by potentially distracting details. Students may be cognitively overwhelmed by the complexity and distracted by irrelevant details. Such distractions, however, are an ever-present reality for practitioners of STEM disciplines, so the potential gain for students is to face the challenges and complexities and determine which warrant further attention and inquiry (Ford 2010; Ford and Forman 2006). Second, students need to draw on and build their knowledge and skills, and develop facility with representations, in individual disciplines at the same time they are making connections across disciplines. Third, students need opportunities and supports for productive embodied cognitive and social interactions that support their learning.

IMPLICATIONS FOR THE DESIGN OF APPROACHES TO INTEGRATED STEM EDUCATION

Research findings on integration converge with those on cognitive, social, and embodied learning processes to highlight the importance of designing integrated experiences that explicitly support students in building knowledge and skill both within and across disciplines. These strategies for instructional design also need to take into account the collaborative nature of learning and include guidance for structuring students' interactions with their peers and teachers. In the next sections, we discuss principles for the design of integrated STEM learning experiences, including: making integration explicit, attending to the students' disciplinary knowledge, attending to the social aspects of learning, and supporting the development of interest and identity.

Making Integration Explicit

Observation studies in K–12 classrooms show that pedagogical practices aimed at fostering integration are quite rare. Analyses of K–12 engineering curricula, for example, reveal that, although many valuable STEM concepts are presented to students in rich contexts, the explicit integration of mathematics and science concepts is not common (NAE and NRC 2009; Prevost et al. 2009; Welty et al. 2008). These analyses also show that, although many mathematics and science concepts are present in the curriculum, they tend to be embedded in the activities (e.g., Redish and Smith 2008), CAD software, measurement instruments, and computational tools used in the classroom.

Explicit integration seems to be particularly rare in entry-level courses; more advanced engineering classes, such as digital electronics, typically support explicit integration, albeit for a smaller and more sophisticated pool of students (Prevost et al. 2010).

Students are less likely to make connections on their own without explicit integration (Graesser et al. 2008; NRC 2001). Its absence is probably not intentional but rather due to teachers' and curriculum developers' highly refined knowledge of the material. Similarly, instructors and curriculum developers shape their teaching by their more advanced understanding and experience an "expert blind spot" (Nathan and Petrosino 2003): they spontaneously see the deep connections and expect that their students will, too.

But one of the most important roles of a STEM instructor is to explicitly draw students' attention to deep structural relations shared across objects and representations. Without this support, students often fail to identify which components of a representation or problem solution matter (Ainsworth et al. 2002; Bottge et al. 2007). Another approach is to design instructional experiences that compel students to develop conjectures about which relations matter and ways to test these conjectures (e.g., Lehrer and Lesh 2013 re designing mathematical modeling).

The lack of explicit integration in STEM instruction is also problematic because studies show that students do not spontaneously integrate what they learn across representations and materials or across multi-day lessons, so integration cannot simply be assumed to take place simply because of temporal or spatial juxtaposition (Kozma 2003; Nathan et al., 2013; Walkington et al., in press). Analyses of project- and problem-based STEM units in both technical education and college-preparatory courses show that deep connecting concepts that thread through formal lectures laden with symbolic notation and graphs are not readily applied by students as the projects move from design to simulation, fabrication and construction, and testing and phases of analysis and redesign (Nathan et al. 2011). These connections must be articulated and maintained by instructors throughout the course (Kanter 2010). Once connections are made—most often by teachers but occasionally by peers—students are better able to see the phases of project-based units as a cohesive whole and their performance often improves (Richland et al. 2007). Furthermore, operating with these connections in mind can actually change students' perceptions of the project materials and representations and how they communicate about them (Nathan et al. 2013).

Attending to Students' Disciplinary Knowledge

Because integrated approaches are intended to help students both deepen their disciplinary knowledge and make connections across disciplines, instructional designers need to understand how students connect ideas even within a discipline (Nordine et al. 2010) and then consider how to help them use their discipline-specific knowledge in the integrated context. Connecting ideas across disciplines (Stevens et al. 2005) may be challenging as students are unlikely to cue their normative disciplinary ideas in disparate contexts. They need explicit support to elicit scientific or mathematical ideas in an engineering or technological design context, to connect those ideas productively, and to reorganize their ideas in ways that come to reflect normative, scientific ones.

A number of integrated programs that use design as a context for learning science have incorporated scaffolding supports to help students connect normative science ideas to their designs (Fortus et al. 2004; Kolodner et al. 2003). Additional supports may be necessary to help students express and rework their understanding of scientific ideas. For instance, Puntambekar and Kolodner (2005) used explicit prompts in design diaries and whole-class pinup sessions and presentations to encourage students to justify and articulate the science behind their design ideas as well as to hear other ideas. Schnittka and Bell (2011) supplemented a design-for-science curriculum with demonstrations that specifically targeted students' alternative conceptions. Using science ideas in troubleshooting is another possible strategy (Crismond and Adams 2012). Supporting students in focusing attention on problematic areas of their prototypes and then using science ideas to offer possible explanations of why the problem may be occurring can be a powerful context for the use of these ideas in improving designs (Crismond and Adams 2012). In sum, typical design-for-science activities need additional, targeted scaffolding for students to explicitly connect and sort through their science ideas in the context of their design activities.

Developers of design-based curricula need to make sure that abstract knowledge is both motivated from and then applied to the design (Kanter 2010). Students are also likely to need explicit support in projecting backward in time to reflect on the process of connecting the normative science idea to their design. Such reflections are rare in design activities (Walkington et al., in press) but are likely the primary mechanism for students' grasping the strength and centrality of normative science and mathematics ideas.

Attending to the Social Aspects of Learning[3]

Social approaches to learning and cognitive development offer several important ideas for the design of integrated STEM education. As noted earlier in this chapter, the social elements of a learning activity include the learners and their interactions, the teacher's guidance and support in directing learning, the activity itself, and the materials or tools used.

The social components of the learning environment are interdependent, and learning depends on their coordination, but they have received little attention in research. Two key questions are:

- What social processes will promote individual learning in integrated STEM education?
- Can these social processes be implemented in systematic and effective ways?

In the following sections we discuss social elements of learning that are possible directions for future research and that can usefully inform the design of integrated STEM instruction.

Social Arrangement

The use of small social groups in integrated STEM learning is consistent with the theoretical view that learning and cognitive development do not reside separately in the child or in the social context, but in the child-in-social-context. The ways in which participants are involved in problem-solving activities is as important to the design of integrated STEM education as the problems themselves. Group activity needs to be designed to allow and encourage children to be active and contributing members. Social arrangements that use group work simply to lure children into the activities, use individual group members to manage (offload) elements of the problem, or do not allow ample time for individual or group work when needed or desired do not promote learning.

---

[3] This section is based on a commissioned paper by Mary Gauvain, University of California, Riverside.

Social Process

Even with well-designed activities or groups, people cannot just be assigned to them with the expectation that social processes that foster learning will automatically emerge. Conversation, argument, note taking, and other recording and review activities should be part of the integrated STEM design. These techniques foster active participation by individual group members and help engage both the mind and the body (sensory and motor systems) in learning. Use of a distributed learning approach in which each group member has a meaningful role may produce more uniform engagement of all participants. Rotating roles and regular peer instructional exchanges are important. In addition, the design should include explicit and specific learning outcomes for individuals in relation to the various aspects of the problem and clear means of assessing these gains, both within and outside the group. A distributed learning approach may also be useful for addressing learning issues related to equity and diversity in the classroom setting. Such approaches can create opportunities for learners to observe and engage with other learners as competent and contributing members of the group.

Role of the Teacher

Teachers can provide effective instruction by engaging students in learning with the support and guidance they need (without doing the thinking for them). They should be attentive to learners' needs as they work with them, individually and in groups, and be able to ensure the positive and productive involvement of all as well as facilitate engagement when group work breaks down. They should also have techniques to guide (or redirect, as necessary) learners toward achieving the learning goal. It is important to recognize that requests for help are evidence of active engagement in learning and not an indication of a deficit. Teachers also need to be prepared to offer hints that steer individual and group learners toward insight into problems without being overly directive.

As learning in integrated contexts becomes more commonplace, further research may yield findings that aid teachers in understanding students' development, as exemplified by research on learning progressions in mathematics and in science education.

Supporting the Development of Interest and Identity[4]

As explained in Chapter 3, while there is little or no research that explicitly examines how to design integrated STEM learning experiences to support interest, there is research that describes features of learning environments in general that promote the development of interest. Azevedo (2006), for example, identified four factors that contributed to the development and deepening of students' interest in grades 7–12 during their work with image processing in a computer laboratory:

- a general feeling of competence;
- the features of activities, including whether they allow the students to express their competence;
- enough time both to complete activities and to initiate activities that students come up with themselves; and
- the flexibility of the learning environment.

Competence here reflects the learners' knowing that they will be able to be successful in the activities and that they have the necessary support to be successful. Azevedo (2006) also points to the importance of designing the activity in such a way that it provides opportunities for feedback that builds competence.

The need for learners to have enough time both to complete activities and to initiate activities they select is critical, according to Azevedo (2006); adequate time not only ensures that the activity is completed but also makes it possible for the learner to engage in "personal excursions," a basis for developing interest. He explains that personal excursions are typically aligned with the planned activity and prompt the learner to make connections between present and previous activity, ask questions, and/or seek resources that contribute to deepening understanding (see Flum and Kaplan 2006).

Research has also demonstrated the importance of the following design elements for integrated STEM education:

- Interactions with others (Barron et al. 2009; Pressick-Kilborn and Walker 2002; Renninger and Hidi 2002)—educators, workshop facilitators, parents, peers—provide models of how one engages with others and works on the problem solving of STEM content.

---

[4] This section is based on commissioned papers by Angela Calabrese Barton, Michigan State University, and K. Ann Renninger, Swarthmore College.

They can be a source of encouragement, stimulating feelings of competence and continued engagement,.

- Triggers of interest (Durik and Harackiewicz 2007; Renninger and Hidi 2002; see also Renninger and Su 2012) vary from earlier to later phases of interest: (1) real-world connections and connections to prior experiences and instruction are important for learners in earlier phases of interest development, whereas the opportunity to continue to be challenged to think about the content is important to learners in later phases of interest (Renninger 2010); (2) in earlier phases of interest puzzles and group work can trigger interest, and personalization and meaningfulness may sustain it (e.g., Palmer 2004, 2009; Mitchell 1993).
- More open learning environments such as project- and problem-based learning sustain interested engagement and enable it to develop (e.g., Renninger and Riley, in press;). Opportunities for sustained inquiry ground student participation in other STEM practices as well. For example, elementary students' inventions and revisions of representations and models of ecosystem functioning are motivated by their questions about local ecologies (Lehrer and Schauble 2012; Manz 2012), and students' disposition to generalize and seek invariants in light of change about mathematical systems is nurtured by sustained opportunities to pose mathematical questions and conduct investigations related to them (Lehrer et al. 2012).

Although there is very little work on identity development and integrated STEM, studies of the development of identity in science offer insights. For example, traditional approaches to science often favor aspects of a science identity that are more reflective of schooling than of science itself, thereby limiting engagement of some youth with strong science identities and rich knowledge based on nonschool experiences (Bricker and Bell 2012; Brickhouse 2001; Brickhouse et al. 2000; Brickhouse and Potter 2001).

In one case study, Carlone and colleagues (2011) examined what it meant to be scientific in two 4th-grade classes taught by teachers who were both committed to reform-based science instructional practices. Students in both classrooms achieved at similar levels and expressed positive attitudes toward science learning, but differences emerged in what it meant to be recognized as a smart science student. One of the teachers allowed for and supported a wide range of science practices, fostering a classroom culture in which scientific expertise carried a range of meanings. The other teacher held more narrowly defined views of science practice, thus limiting the opportunity for all students in the class to engage actively.

In contrast, an ethnographic study of an urban magnet high school (Buxton 2005) shows how students resisted and transformed the identity of the "preferred student" and in doing so impacted the cultural, institutional, and structural features of their school. The students' interactions with each other and with their teachers led to the development of new tasks and relationships that helped to change perceptions of what counted as a "good science student." Teachers became more open to redefining what counted as successful student work, and course scheduling patterns were changed to address students' needs and interests.

These two studies suggest that teachers play a dynamic role in the development of science identity. In the comparative study by Carlone and colleagues (2011), the teacher who privileged the sharing and vetting of ideas and tools over securing the right answer created more spaces for students to try out being scientific. The implication is that, even when teachers commit to enacting reform-based science, without explicit attention to the ways they support different possible identities it may be difficult to foster the kinds of identities that support meaningful learning.

Looking across studies of science learning, there is evidence that classroom interventions and design experiments grounded in reform-based curriculum/pedagogy and intended to explicitly incorporate students' identities in instruction can positively impact learning and identity. Calabrese Barton and Tan (2009) report that one teacher's approach to a reform-based inquiry unit on dynamic equilibrium and the human body led students not only to learn the relevant concepts but also to exhibit strong science identities. Using a design experiment approach, the authors collaborated with the teacher and a small group of students to design lesson extensions that incorporated students' existing knowledge. Use of the students' own knowledge positioned them as experts and positively impacted how they viewed themselves and ultimately participated in class. Thus the design of the learning environment, including how resources are made accessible and legitimized, norms, routines, and expectations, all play crucial roles in how identities are formed.

Youth who engage in project-based investigations with local significance, codeveloping research questions and identifying connections to the work of practicing scientists and engineers, develop positive science identities (Calabrese Barton 1998; Furman and Calabrese Barton 2006; Rahm and Ash 2008). A number of studies show that when youth engage in science projects, they activate a combination of traditionally scientific and non-scientific resources, and this engagement supports them in being recognized as experts, as successful in school/science, while they maintain cultural allegiance.

But the research has focused on programs in which participation is voluntary and long-term. Given the time scale of identity development (see next section) long-term engagement could be a critical component of these programs.

Summary

Looking across the literatures on instruction that supports development of interest and identity, a few key features emerge. It is important to provide learning opportunities that make students feel competent and give them opportunities to express that competence. Learning experiences that allow flexibility and choice for students and that make connections to the real world are also important. Project- and problem-based experiences seem to be especially effective in supporting the development of interest and identity, suggesting that integrated STEM experiences can be powerful tools for building students' interest and identity in STEM fields.

In sum, integrated STEM can provide opportunities for students to productively engage in STEM in ways that spark their interest and transform their identity. But the research base is sparse, particularly on the subject of designing integrated STEM experiences to intentionally support interest and identity.

CONCLUSIONS

Disciplinary integration can support learning because basic qualities of cognition favor connected concepts and representations, so they are associated with other knowledge and grounded in familiar experiences. In some cases, however, the presentation of concepts in the context of activities that integrate multiple disciplines can impede comprehension and learning because of the cognitive processing demands associated with split attention. Moreover, there are substantial differences in how different disciplines generate and validate knowledge, and it is not clear when these differences matter for learning and when they do not.

Work on complex, real-world problems, which almost always call on multiple disciplines, can support both short-term learning and longer-term application or transfer to new contexts. However, these desired outcomes are not a given and depend on factors related to the design and implementation of the learning experience as well as the teacher's ability to effectively support student problem-solving efforts.

Integrated STEM experiences should be designed so that they support students' development of knowledge and practices in individual disciplines and their ability to recognize and make connections across disciplines. STEM curricula should also attend to discipline-specific learning progressions; if the learning goals of one discipline are primary, the knowledge and skills of other disciplines should be integrated into the curriculum with the learning progressions of that discipline in mind.

STEM connections that may appear obvious to teachers, curriculum developers, and disciplinary experts often are not obvious to novice learners and cannot be assumed to occur simply because certain concepts and practices are introduced at the same time or place. Integrated STEM instruction needs to make connections explicit to students through scaffolding, sufficient opportunities to engage in activities that address connected ideas, and other approaches described in this chapter.

REFERENCES

Ainsworth, S.E., P.A. Bibby, and D.J. Wood. 2002. Examining the effects of different multiple representational systems in learning primary mathematics. Journal of the Learning Sciences 11(1): 25–62.

Anderson, J.R. 1996. ACT: A simple theory of complex cognition. American Psychologist 51(4): 355–365.

Anderson, J.R., D. Bothell, M.D. Byrne, S. Douglass, C. Lebiere, and Y. Qin. 2004. An integrated theory of the mind. Psychological Review 111(4):1036–1060.

Azevedo, F.S. 2006. Personal excursions: Investigating the dynamics of student engagement. International Journal of Computers for Mathematical Learning 11:57–98.

Barron, B., C. Kennedy-Martin, L. Takeuchi, and R. Fithian. 2009. Parents as learning partners in the development of technological fluency. International Journal of Learning and Media 1(2):55–77.

Bobis, J., J. Sweller, and M. Cooper, 1993. Cognitive load effects in a primary school geometry task. Learning and Instruction 3:1–21.

Bolger, M.S., M. Kobiela, P.J. Weinberg, and R. Lehrer. 2012. Children's mechanistic reasoning. Cognition and Instruction 30(2):170–206.

Bolger, M.S., M.A. Kobiela, P.J. Weinberg, and R. Lehrer. 2010. Embodied experiences within an engineering curriculum. Proceedings of the 9th International Conference of the Learning Sciences (ICLS 2010), Vol. 1, 706–713. International Society of the Learning Sciences: Chicago, IL.

Bolger, M.S., P.J. Weinberg, M.A. Kobiela, R.J. Rouse, and R. Lehrer. 2011, April. Embodied experiences as a resource for children's mechanistic and mathematical reasoning in an engineering curriculum. Paper presented at the 2011 Meeting of the National Association for Research in Science Teaching, Orlando, FL.

Bottge, B.A., E. Rueda, P.T. LaRoque, R.C. Serlin, and J. Kwon. 2007. Integrating reform-oriented math instruction in special education settings. Learning Disabilities Research and Practice 22:96–109.

Bricker, L.A., and P. Bell. 2012. "GodMode is his video game name": Situating learning and identity in structures of social practice. Cultural Studies of Science Education 28:1–20. doi:10.1007/s11422–012–9410–6.

Brickhouse, N.W., and J.T. Potter. 2001. Young women's scientific identity formation in an urban context. Journal of Research in Science Teaching 38:965–980. doi: 10.1002/tea.1041.

Brickhouse, N.W. 2001. Embodying science: A feminist perspective on learning. Journal of Research in Science Teaching 38(3):282–295.

Brickhouse, N.W., P. Lowery, and K. Schultz. 2000. What kind of a girl does science? The construction of school science identities. Journal of Research in Science Teaching 37:441–458. doi: 10.1002/(SICI)1098–2736200005)37:5<441::AID-TEA4>3.0.CO;2–3.

Buxton, C. 2005. Creating a culture of academic success in an urban science and math magnet high school. Science Education 89(3):392–417.

Calabrese Barton, A. 1998. Teaching science with homeless children: Pedagogy, representation, and identity. Journal of Research in Science Teaching 35:379–394.

Calabrese Barton, A., and E. Tan. 2009. Funds of knowledge, discourses and hybrid space. Journal of Research in Science Teaching 46(1):50–73.

Calabrese Barton, A., and E. Tan. 2010a. We be burnin': Agency, identity and learning. Journal of the Learning Sciences 19:187–229.

Calabrese Barton, A., and E. Tan. 2010b. The new green roof: Activism, science and greening the community. Journal of Canadian Journal of Science, Mathematics and Technology Education 10(3):207–222.

Carlone, H.B., J. Haun-Frank, and A. Webb. 2011. Assessing equity beyond knowledge- and skills based outcomes: A comparative ethnography of two fourth-grade reform-based science classrooms. Journal of Research in Science Teaching 48(5):459–485.

Case, R., and Y. Okamoto. 1996. The role of central conceptual structures in the development of children's thought. Monographs of the Society for Research in Child Development 61(1–2, Serial No. 246).

Chao, S.J., J. W. Stigler, and J.A. Woodward. 2000. The effects of physical materials on kindergartners' learning of number concepts. Cognition and Instruction 18(3):285–316.

Chandler, P., and J. Sweller. 1992. The split-attention effect as a factor in the design of instruction. British Journal of Educational Psychology 62:233–246.

Chandler, P., and J. Sweller. 1996. Cognitive load while learning to use a computer program. Applied Cognitive Psychology 10:151–170.

Chi, M.T.H., P.J. Feltovich, and R. Glaser. 1981. Categorization and representation of physics problems by experts and novices. Cognitive Science 5(2):121–152.

Clements, D.H. 2000. Concrete manipulatives, concrete ideas. Contemporary Issues in Early Childhood 1(1):5–60.

Crismond, D., and R. Adams. 2012. The informed design teaching and learning matrix. Journal of Engineering Education 101(4):738–797.

Cronbach, L., and R. Snow. 1977. Aptitudes and instructional methods: A handbook for research on interactions. New York: Irvington.

Danish, J.A., and N. Enyedy. 2007. Negotiated representational mediators: How young children decide what to include in their science representations. Science Education 91:1–35.

Dehaene, S., E. Spelke, P. Pinel, R. Stanescu, and S. Tsivkin. 1999. Sources of mathematical thinking: Behavioral and brain-imaging evidence. Science 284:970–974.

diSessa, A.A. 2004. Meta-representation: Native competence and targets for instruction. Cognition and Instruction 22(3):293–331.

Durik, A., and J.M. Harackiewicz. 2007. Different strokes for different folks: How individual interest moderates the effects of situational factors on task interest. Journal of Educational Psychology 99(3):597–610.

Ellis, S.A., and M. Gauvain. 1992. Social and cultural influences on children's collaborative interactions. In L. T. Winegar and J. Valsiner (Eds.), Children's development within social context: Research and methodology (Vol. 2, pp. 155–180). Hillsdale, NJ: Erlbaum.

Ericsson, K.A., W.G. Chase, and S. Faloon. 1980. Acquisition of a memory skill. Science 208:1181–1182.

Flum, H., and A. Kaplan. 2006. Exploratory orientation as an educational goal. Educational Psychologist 41(2):9–110.

Ford, M.J. 2010. Critique in academic disciplines and active learning of academic content. Cambridge Journal of Education 40(3):265–280.

Ford, M.J., and E.A. Forman. 2006. Refining disciplinary learning in classroom contexts. Review of Research in Education 30:1–32.

Fortus, D., R.C. Dershimer, J. Krajcik, R.W. Marx, and R. Mamlok-Naaman. 2004. Design based science and student learning. Journal of Research in Science Teaching 41(10):1081.

Furman, M., and A. Calabrese Barton. 2006. Capturing urban student voices in the creation of a science minidocumentary. Journal of Research on Science Teaching 43:667–694. doi: 10.1002/tea.20164.

Fuson, K.C., W.M. Carroll, and J.V. Drueck. 2000. Achievement results for second and third graders using the Standards-based curriculum Everyday Mathematics. Journal for Research in Mathematics Education 31(3):277-295.

Gauvain, M., and B. Rogoff. 1989. Collaborative problem solving and children's planning skills. Developmental Psychology 25:139–151.

Gauvain, M. 2001. The social context of cognitive development. New York: Guilford.

Gauvain, M. 1992. Social influences on the development of planning in advance and during action. International Journal of Behavioral Development 15:139–151.

Goldstone, R.L., and Y. Sakamoto. 2003. The transfer of abstract principles governing complex adaptive systems. Cognitive Psychology 46(4):414–466.

Goldstone, R.L., and J.. Son. 2005. The transfer of scientific principles using concrete and idealized simulations. Journal of the Learning Sciences 14(1):69–110.

Graesser, A.C., D.F. Halpern, and M. Hakel. 2008. 25 principles of learning. Washington: Task Force on Lifelong Learning at Work and at Home. Available at www.psyc.memphis.edu/learning/whatweknow/index.shtml (retrieved July 29, 2013).

Greeno, J.G., and R.P. Hall. 1997. Practicing representation. Phi Delta Kappan 78(5):361–367.

Griffin, S., R. Case, and R. Siegler. 1994. Rightstart: Providing the central conceptual prerequisites for first formal learning of arithmetic to students at risk for school failure. In K. McGilly (Ed.), Classroom lessons: Integrating cognitive theory and classroom practice (pp. 24–49). Cambridge, MA: MIT Press.

Kaminski, J.A., V.M. Sloutsky, and A.F. Heckler. 2006a. Effects of concreteness on representation: An explanation for differential transfer. Proceedings of the XXVIII Annual Conference of the Cognitive Science Society, pp. 1581–1586. Mahwah, NJ: Erlbaum.

Kaminski, J.A., V.M. Sloutsky, and A.F. Heckler. 2006b. Do children need concrete instantiations to learn an abstract concept? Proceedings of the XXVIII Annual Conference of the Cognitive Science Society, pp. 411–416. Mahwah, NJ: Erlbaum.

Kaminski, J.A., V.M. Sloutsky, and A. Heckler. 2009. Transfer of mathematical knowledge: The portability of generic instantiations. Child Development Perspectives 3(3):151–155.

Kanter, D.E. 2010. Doing the project and learning the content: Designing project-based science curricula for meaningful understanding. Science Education 94(3):525–551.

Karabenick, S.A., and R.S. Newman. 2006. Help seeking in academic settings: Goals, groups, and contexts. Mahwah, NJ: Erlbaum.

Kirsh, D., and P. Maglio. 1994. On distinguishing epistemic from pragmatic action. Cognitive Science 18(4):513–549.

Koedinger, K.R., A.C. Corbett, and C. Perfetti. 2012. The Knowledge-Learning-Instruction (KLI) framework: Bridging the science-practice chasm to enhance robust student learning. Cognitive Science 36(5):757–798.

Kolodner, J.L., P.J. Camp, D. Crismond, B. Fasse, J. Gray, J. Holbrook, S. Puntambekar, and M. Ryan. 2003. Problem-based learning meets case-based reasoning in the middle-school science classroom: Putting Learning by Design™ into practice. Journal of the Learning Sciences 12(4):495–547. doi: 10.1207/S15327809JLS1204_2.

Kontra, C.E., S. Goldin-Meadow, and S.L. Beilock. 2012. Embodied learning across the life span. Topics in Cognitive Science 4:731–739.

Kozma, R. 2003. The material features of multiple representations and their cognitive and social affordances for science understanding. Learning and Instruction 13:205–226.

Kozma, R., E. Chin, J. Russell, and N. Marx. 2000. The role of representations and tools in the chemistry laboratory and their implications for chemistry learning. Journal of the Learning Sciences 9(3):105–144.

Lancy, D.F., S. Gaskins, and J. Bock. (Eds.). 2010. The anthropology of learning in childhood. Lanham, MD: Alta-Mira Press.

Latour, B. 1999. Pandora's hope. Essays on the reality of science studies. Cambridge, MA: Harvard University Press.

Lehrer, R., and R. Lesh. 2013. Mathematical learning. In I.B. Weiner (Ed.), Handbook of psychology, 2nd ed. (pp. 283–320). New York: Wiley.

Lehrer, R., and L. Schauble. 2012. Seeding evolutionary thinking by engaging children in modeling its foundations. Science Education 96(4):701–724.

Lehrer, R., M. Kobiela, and P. Weinberg. 2013. Cultivating inquiry about space in a middle school mathematics classroom. International Journal on Mathematics Education (ZDM) 45(3):365–376.

Light, P., and K. Littleton. 1999. Social processes in children's learning. Cambridge, England: Cambridge University Press.

Manz, E. 2012. Understanding the codevelopment of modeling practice and ecological knowledge. Science Education 96(6):1071–1105.

Martin, T., and D.L. Schwartz. 2005. Physically distributed learning: Adapting and reinterpreting physical environments in the development of fraction concepts. Cognitive Science 29(4):587–625.

Mayer, R.E. 2001. Multimedia Learning. New York: Cambridge University Press.

Mayer, R.E., and R.B. Anderson. 1991. Animations need narrations: An experimental test of a dual-coding hypothesis. Journal of Educational Psychology 83:484–490.

Mayer, R.E., and R.B. Anderson. 1992. The instructive animation: Helping students build connections between words and pictures in multimedia learning. Journal of Educational Psychology 84:444–452.

Mayer, R.E., and R. Moreno. 1998. A split-attention effect in multimedia learning: Evidence for dual processing systems in working memory. Journal of Educational Psychology 90:312–320.

Metz, K.E. 1985. The development of children's problem solving in a gears task: A problem space perspective. Cognitive Science 9(4):431–471.

Miller, G.A. 1956. The magical number seven, plus or minus two: Some limits on our capacity for processing information. Psychological Review 63(2):81–97.

Mitchell, M. 1993. Situational interest: Its multifaceted structure in the secondary school mathematics classroom. Journal of Educational Psychology 85:424–436.

Moreno, R., and R.E. Mayer. 1999. Cognitive principles of multimedia learning: The role of modality and contiguity. Journal of Educational Psychology 91:358–368.

Mwangi, W., and J. Sweller. 1998. Learning to solve compare word problems: The effect of example format and generating self-explanations. Cognition and Instruction 16:173–199.

NAE (National Academy of Engineering) and NRC (National Research Council). 2009. Engineering in K-12 Education: Understanding the status and improving the prospects. Available at www.nap.edu/catalog.php?record_id=12635 (retrieved September 6, 2013).

Nathan, M.J., and K.R. Koedinger. 2000. Teachers' and researchers' beliefs about the development of algebraic reasoning. Journal for Research in Mathematics Education 31:168–190.

Nathan, M.J., and A.J. Petrosino. 2003. expert blind spot among preservice teachers. American Educational Research Journal 40(4):905–928.

Nathan, M.J., R. Srisurichan, C. Walkington, M. Wolfram, C. Williams, and M.W. Alibali. 2013. Cohesion as a mechanism of STEM integration. Journal of Engineering Education 102(1):1–216. (Special issue on representation in engineering education.)

Nathan, M.J., M. Wolfgram, R. Srisurichan, and M.W. Alibali. 2011. Model engagements in precollege engineering: Tracking mathematics and science across symbols, sketches, software, silicon, and wood. Proceedings of the American Society of Engineering Education (ASEE) 2011 (Paper no. AC2011–315 pp. 1–31). Vancouver, BC: ASEE Publications.

Nordine, J., J. Krajcik, and D. Fortus. 2010. Transforming energy instruction in middle school to support integrated understanding and future learning. Science Education 95(4):670–699.

NRC (National Research Council). 2000. How People Learn: Brain, Mind, Experience, and School: Expanded Edition. Washington: The National Academies Press.

NRC. 2001. Knowing What Students Know: The Science and Design of Educational Assessment. Committee on the Foundations of Assessment. J. Pelligrino, N. Chudowsky, and R. Glaser (Eds). Board on Testing and Assessment, Center for Education. Division of Behavioral and Social Sciences and Education. Washington: The National Academies Press.

NRC. 2007. Taking Science to School: Learning and Teaching Science in Grades K-8. Committee on Science Learning, Kindergarten Through Eighth Grade. R. A. Duschl, H. A. Schweingruber, and A. W. Shouse (Eds.). Board on Science Education, Center for Education. Division of Behavioral and Social Sciences and Education. Washington: The National Academies Press.

NRC. 2012. Education for Life and Work: Developing Transferable Knowledge and Skills in the 21st Century. Committee on Defining Deeper Learning and 21st Century Skills. J.W. Pelligrino and M.L. Hilton (Eds.). Board on Testing and Assessment and Board on Science Education, Division of Behavioral and Social Sciences and Education. Washington: The National Academies Press.

Palmer, D.H. 2009. Student interest generated during an inquiry skills lesson. Journal of Research in Science Teaching 46(2):147–165.

Palmer, D.H. 2004. Situational interest and the attitudes towards science of primary teacher education students. International Journal of Science Education 26(7):895–908.

Piaget, J. 1952. The origins of intelligence in children. New York: Norton.

Pressick-Killborn, K., and R. Walker. 2002. The social construction of interest in a learning community. In D.M. McInerney and S. Van Etten (Eds.), Research on sociocultural influences on motivation and learning (Vol. 2, pp. 153–182). Greenwich, CT: Information Age.

Prevost, A., M.J. Nathan, B. Stein, N. Tran, and L.A. Phelps. 2009. Integration of mathematics in pre-college engineering: the search for explicit connections. Proceedings of the American Society of Engineering Education (ASEE) 2009 (Paper no. AC 2009–1790, pp. 1–27). Austin, TX: ASEE Publications.

Prevost, A., M.J. Nathan, B. Stein, and L.A. Phelps. 2010. The enacted curriculum: A video based analysis of instruction and learning in high school engineering classrooms. Proceedings of the American Society of Engineering Education (ASEE) 2010 (Paper no. AC 2010–2011). Louisville, KY: ASEE Publications.

Puntambekar, S., and J.L. Kolodner. 2005. Toward implementing distributed scaffolding: Helping students learn science from design. Journal of Research in Science Teaching 42(2):185–217.

Rahm, J. 2008. Urban youths' hybrid identity projects in science practices at the margin: A look inside a school-museum-scientist partnership project and an afterschool science program. Cultural Studies of Science Education, 3(1):97–121.

Rahm, J., and D. Ash. 2008 Learning environments at the margin: Case studies of disenfranchised youth doing science in an aquarium and an after-school program. Learning Environments Research 11(1):49–62. doi: 10.1007/s10984-007-9037-9.

Rau, M.A., R. Scheines, V. Aleven, and N. Rummel. 2013. Does conceptual understanding enhance acquisition of fluency—or vice versa? Searching for models to investigate mediators. In S.K. D'Mello, R.A. Calvo, and A. Olney (Eds.), Proceedings of the 6th International Conference on Educational Data Mining (EDM 2013) (pp. 161–169).

Redish, E.F., and K.A. Smith. 2008. Looking beyond content: Skill development for engineers. Journal of Engineering Education 97:295–307.

Renninger, K.A. 2010. Working with and cultivating interest, self-efficacy, and self-regulation. In D. Preiss and R. Sternberg (Eds.), Innovations in educational psychology: Perspectives on learning, teaching and human development (pp. 107–138). New York: Springer.

Renninger, K.A., and N. Granott. 2005. The process of scaffolding in learning and development. New Ideas in Psychology 23:111–114.

Renninger, K.A., and S. Hidi. 2002. Student interest and achievement: Developmental issues raised by a case study. In A. Wigfield and J. S. Eccles (Eds.), Development of achievement motivation (pp. 173–195). New York: Academic Press.

Renninger, K.A., and R. Lipstein. 2006. Come si sviluppa l'interesse per la scrittura; cosa vogliono gli studenti e di cosa hanno bisogno? [Developing interest for writing: What do students want and what do students need?] Età Evolutiva 44(84):65–83.

Renninger, K.A., and K. Riley. 2013. Interest, cognition, and the case of L– and science. In S. Kreitler (Ed.). Cognition and motivation: Forging an interdisciplinary perspective (pp. 352–382). New York: Cambridge University Press.

Renninger, K.A., and S. Su. 2012. Interest and its development. In R. Ryan (Ed.), Oxford Handbook of Motivation (pp. 167-187). New York: Oxford University Press.

Richland, L.E., O. Zur, and K.J. Holyoak. 2007. Cognitive supports for analogy in the mathematics classroom. Science 316:1128–1129.

Schnittka, C., and R. Bell. 2011. Engineering design and conceptual change in science: Addressing thermal energy and heat transfer in eighth grade. International Journal of Science Education 33(13):1861–1887.

Schwartz, D. 1995. The emergence of abstract representations in dyad problem solving. Journal of the Learning Sciences 4(3):321–354.

Serlin, R.C., and J.R. Levin. 1980. Identifying regions of significance in aptitude by treatment research. American Educational Research Journal 17:389–399.

Slavin, R. 1983. When does cooperative learning increase student achievement? Psychological Bulletin 94:429–445.

Sloutsky, V.M., J.A. Kaminski, and A.F. Heckler. 2005. The advantage of simple symbols for learning and transfer. Psychonomic Bulletin and Review 12(3):508–513.

Stenning, K., and J. Oberlander. 1995. A cognitive theory of graphical and linguistic reasoning: Logic and implementation. Cognitive Science 19:97–140.

Stevens, R., S. Wineburg, L.R. Herrenkohl, and P. Bell. 2005. Comparative understanding of school subjects: Past, present, and future. Review of Educational Research 75(2):125–157.

Sweller, J., P. Chandler, P. Tierney, and M. Cooper. 1990. Cognitive load and selective attention as factors in the structuring of technical material. Journal of Experimental Psychology: General 119:176–192.

Sweller, J., J.J.G. van Merrienboer, and F.G.W.C. Paas. 1998. Cognitive architecture and instructional design. Educational Psychology Review 10:251–296.

Tabachneck, H. 1992. Computational differences in mental representations: Effects of mode of data presentation on reasoning and understanding. Doctoral Dissertation. Carnegie Mellon University.

Tabachneck, H.J.M., A.M. Leonardo, and H.A. Simon. 1994. How does an expert use a graph? A model of visual and verbal inferencing in economics. Proceedings of the 16th Annual Conference of the Cognitive Science Society, pp. 842–847.

Uttal, D.H., K.V. Scudder, and J.S. DeLoache. 1997. Manipulatives as symbols: A new perspective on the use of concrete objects to teach mathematics. Journal of Applied Developmental Psychology 18(1):37–54.

Vygotsky, L.S. 1978. Mind in Society: The Development of Higher Psychological Processes. M. Cole, V. John-Steiner, S. Scribner, and E. Souberman (Eds.). Cambridge, MA: Harvard University Press.

Walkington, C.A., M.J. Nathan, M. Wolfgram, M.W. Alibali, and R. Srisurichan. In press. Bridges and barriers to constructing conceptual cohesion across modalities and temporalities: Challenges of STEM integration in the precollege engineering classroom. In J. Strobel, S. Purzer and M. Cardella (Eds.), Engineering in PreCollege Settings: Research into Practice. Rotterdam, Netherlands: Sense Publishers.

Welty, K., L. Katehi, G. Pearson, and M. Feder. 2008. Analysis of K–12 engineering education curricula in the United States: A preliminary report. American Society for Engineeering Education, Proceedings of the 2008 Annual Conference and Exposition.

Wood, D.J., and D. Middleton. 1975. A study of assisted problem solving. British Journal of Psychology 66:181–191.

Wood, D.J., J.S. Bruner, and G. Ross. 1976. The role of tutoring in problem solving. Journal of Child Psychology and Psychiatry 17(2):89–100.

Wood, D.J., H. Wood, and D. Middleton. 1978. An experimental evaluation of four face-to-face teaching strategies. International Journal of Behavioral Development 2:131–147.

5

Context for Implementing Integrated STEM

I n the two preceding chapters we reviewed research that can inform the development of effective integrated STEM programs (Chapter 3) and, based on this research, identified strategies for designing programs (Chapter 4). In this chapter we consider the broader context for implementing integrated STEM education, taking account of factors at the school, district, state, and national levels. We examine three elements of the education system that can advance or limit opportunities for providing integrated STEM: standards, assessment, and teacher education and professional development, including the importance of collaboration. We also briefly touch on other contextual factors that might affect efforts to implement integrated STEM education.

STANDARDS

The most recent standards for mathematics and science education, the *Common Core State Standards for Mathematics* (CCSSM; NGACPB 2010) and the *Next Generation Science Standards* (NGSS; NRC 2013a), can support efforts to make connections across the disciplines. The CCSSM call for students to use mathematics in applied contexts and identify practices in mathematics that can link to those of science and engineering. The NGSS explicitly include practices and core ideas from engineering and technology. The increased focus on applications of math and science concepts, the emphasis on practices in mathematics, science, and engineering, and the addition of engineering design as a central aspect of the NGSS all provide strong support for more integration of STEM in math and science curriculum and teaching. Likewise, the *Standards for Technological Literacy: Content for the Study of Technology* (ITEEA 2000) spell out learning goals related to engineering design and emphasize the need for students to understand technology's connections to science, engineering, and mathematics.

The committee recognizes that not all states will adopt the CCSSM or the NGSS. Even so, the standards have the potential to influence approaches to mathematics and science education, even in states that do not formally adopt them. The standards call for the engagement of students in authentic tasks that require integration across the STEM disciplines and support for the development and application of conceptual knowledge and reasoning.

The NGSS, based on the NRC's *Framework for K–12 Science Education* (NRC 2012), identify eight practices in science and engineering that may serve as starting points for integrating science, engineering, and mathematics. Engineering practices are described alongside scientific practices, several of which offer opportunities to link to mathematics, including "modeling" and "using mathematics and computational thinking." The *Framework* and NGSS also describe core ideas related to engineering design. The goal of including practices and ideas related to engineering, technology, and applications of science is to help students understand the similarities and differences between science and engineering by making the connections between them explicit (NRC 2012).

The *Framework* and NGSS also outline seven crosscutting concepts relevant to both science and engineering; two of these concepts—"Patterns and Scale, Proportion, and Quantity"—have clear links to mathematics. The NGSS identify connections to elements of the CCSSM and provide examples (Appendix L) of the use of mathematics in the context of science.

The standards for mathematical practice outlined in the CCSSM also have potential links to the scientific and engineering practices in the NGSS (see Table 5-1). For example, one of the standards, "Using appropriate tools strategically," calls for students to select tools appropriate for solving a mathematical problem; the tools can include computer software as well as "hard" technology. Knowledge of what the technologies can and cannot do in a given situation and how to use estimation are essential for the effective use of technology in mathematics. For high school students, "modeling" is a conceptual category in CCSSM; as described in the overview of this cat-

TABLE 5-1 Mathematical Practices in the *Common Core State Standards for Mathematics* and Scientific and Engineering Practices in the *Next Generation Science Standards*

Mathematical Practices	Scientific and Engineering Practices
1. Make sense of problems and persevere in solving them	1. Ask questions and define problems
2. Reason abstractly and quantitatively	2. Develop and use models
3. Construct viable arguments and critique the reasoning of others	3. Plan and carry out investigations
4. Model with mathematics	4. Analyze and interpret data
5. Use appropriate tools strategically	5. Use mathematics and computational thinking
6. Attend to precision	6. Construct explanations and design solutions
7. Look for and make use of structure	7. Engage in argument from evidence
8. Looking for and expressing regularity in repeated reasoning	8. Obtain, evaluate, and communicate information

egory, the modeling cycle can also be viewed as an engineering design cycle: It involves making choices, assumptions, and approximations. The use of technology is also inherent in modeling; computer-assisted design programs and 3D modeling applications, for example, are tools that are often used in the modeling process.

A potential challenge of taking advantage of the apparent overlap in the practices identified in the CCSSM and NGSS is clarification for students of the similarities and differences in the two disciplines (e.g., Davidson et al. 1998). For example, argumentation in mathematics differs from argumentation in science. Students will need to develop the ability to engage in argumentation in each and to understand how the two types of argument differ. Whether skill in one form of argumentation can enhance skill in another is an open, empirical question.

In addition to standards for mathematical practice, the CCSSM identify concepts in 11 domains and describe what students should understand in these domains at each grade level. Many of the concepts are critical to science and engineering. For example, according to CCSSM standard 8.G.4, 8th-grade students are expected to understand congruence and similarity in mathematics using physical models, transparencies, or geometry software. This standard may support achievement of the 8th-grade endpoint in engineering design outlined in the *Framework*, to consider possible constraints on design solutions (ETS1.A). Students in 8th grade are also expected to learn to investigate patterns of association in bivariate data (CCSSM, 8.SP.1). This concept links to the crosscutting concept of patterns in the *Framework* and NGSS and is important to scientific investigation and engineering design.

One challenge of implementing both the CCSSM and NGSS is to ensure the development of discipline-specific knowledge while also supporting connections across STEM. As reported in Chapter 3, analyses of math and science integration have found fewer benefits for math outcomes compared to science outcomes (e.g., Hartzler 2000). Therefore, as the CCSSM and NGSS are implemented, research on approaches to integrated STEM education will be necessary to enhance learning outcomes for all the disciplines. For example, students in high school are expected to apply geometric concepts in modeling situations involving design problems (G.MG.3) and to conduct calculations of density based on area and volume (G.MG.2)The teacher could use a science- and engineering-based lesson to meet these standards with an engineering project in which students use a design-based approach to develop or redesign a fuel-efficient gas tank to meet new environmental standards and minimize human impacts on Earth systems (ESS3.C). A research-based assessment of this integrated lesson would measure improvements in student thinking and learning in mathematics, science, and engineering.

ASSESSMENT

Assessments—from formative assessments at the classroom level to large-scale state assessments for accountability—can limit the extent to which integrated STEM can be incorporated into K–12 education. This is because it is challenging to design assessments that are effective for both discipline-specific and integrated learning. Historically, assessments have focused on concepts in a single discipline, with little attention to disciplinary practices or applications of knowledge. Large-scale assessments used for accountability pose the biggest challenges, although some innovative examples do exist and we touch briefly on those in this section.

Designing Systems of Assessment for Integrated STEM

Assessments of integrated STEM education should be balanced, using multiple levels of assessment (e.g., formative, interim, and summative measures of student performance) in a coherent and continuous manner to address student needs, inform instructional adjustments, and guide long-term educational improvement.[1] A coherent assessment system would connect integrated STEM goals, curricula, and assessments in programs and projects as well as across different levels of the system (classroom, school, district, and state); a continuous system would use multiple assessments over time. Ideally, balanced systems of assessment would be designed to connect evidence of learning from particular integrated STEM programs to more generalized, summative assessments of learning across a range of integrated STEM initiatives. The development of balanced integrated STEM assessment systems will be particularly challenging, because of the many possible permutations of disciplinary knowledge and practices in integrated STEM learning environments. This challenge is exemplified in student performance expectations spelled out in the recently published NGSS, which combine disciplinary core ideas and cross-cutting concepts with scientific practices. Assessment of this "three-dimensional learning" will require tasks that allow students to demonstrate their proficiency with scientific practices and that reflect the connected use of different scientific practices in the context of interconnected disciplinary ideas and crosscutting concepts. A systems approach to assessment will be needed in which a range of assessment strategies are designed to answer different kinds of questions with appropriate degrees of specificity to provide results that complement one another (NRC 2013b).

Current assessments of STEM learning tend to be either standardized tests of content knowledge in the separate disciplines or evaluations of project-specific student performance and/or products in particular interventions. Standardized assessments typically include items only partially aligned with an integrated STEM curriculum or projects, whereas assessments of integrated STEM education tend to measure very specific outcomes, and often details of the tests and their technical quality are not reported. As integrated STEM projects and curricula become more widely implemented, more attention will need to be paid to appropriate uses of data from conventional large-scale tests and to procedures for developing and establishing the technical quality of measures for specific interventions. Research on the reliability and validity of assessments is needed (AERA et al. 1999).

Integrated STEM programs and assessments of them should identify the knowledge and skills to be monitored during learning activities and tested at the culmination of a project (Crismond 2001). An important related consideration is whether the intended integrated STEM outcomes are all at the

---

[1] Balanced assessments are discussed in detail in the NRC report *Systems for State Science Assessment* (NRC 2005).

same grade level for each component discipline or related hierarchically by drawing on knowledge and skills attained in earlier grades.

The design of integrated STEM assessments should be firmly grounded in research from the learning and measurement sciences, which has led to a shift from emphasis on questions about discrete, factual content to questions about interactions among concepts and to tasks that require integration of reasoning and inquiry in the context of significant, applied problems. Thus integrated STEM assessments should feature tasks that provide real-world contexts for using and integrating discipline-specific knowledge while engaging in engineering and scientific practices.

The NRC report *Knowing What Students Know: The Science and Design of Educational Assessment* (NRC 2001) incorporated cognitive research findings into systematic test design frameworks, based on evidence from tasks that enable the observation and measurement of learning. The framework can help to structure and focus both the design of integrated STEM learning activities and the systematic, rigorous assessment of specified learning outcomes.

Integrated STEM assessment designs will vary depending on the purpose of the assessment (e.g., formative monitoring, summative accountability measures) and the particular disciplines to be assessed, but all would specify (1) what would count as evidence of learning and (2) the types of contexts and tasks that would elicit such evidence. Ideally, design of both the activities and assessments would occur simultaneously, accompanied by iterative cross-checking to ensure that the learning activities are designed to promote the specified STEM knowledge and scientific and engineering practices and incorporate systematic assessments of progress in all the target areas. Assessments should also allow for appropriate adjustments in instruction, including the learning supports, or scaffolding, provided to students.

Large-Scale Assessments

Large-scale assessments of students' ability to integrate knowledge and practices related to science, technology, and mathematics are difficult to design, given the possible combinations. At present, the *Technology and Engineering Literacy Framework for the 2014 National Assessment of Educational Progress* (TEL; NAGB 2010) is the primary example of assessment design that integrates technology and engineering. It could be adapted to integrate mathematics and science.

The TEL framework was developed within the constraints typical of large-scale assessments: limited testing time and the need to assess knowledge and skills acquired across a wide range of curriculum programs. It will be administered by computer and the specifications call for short (12-minute) and long (25-minute) scenario-based item sets. An example of a scenario-based item, a simulation of a nuclear reactor developed for the Programme of International Student Assessment (PISA) to assess science, appears in Figure 5-1. It asks students to set the generator valve at a specified level and determine how far the control rods need to be lifted for the power plant to supply a continuous output of megawatts without the safety valve opening. The TEL framework suggests the item can be modified to assess engineering design and systems learning goals, such as analyzing potential hazards of the reactor or determining safe levels of temperature and power.

Two other large-scale assessments that provide examples of tasks to assess integrated STEM learning are the revised advanced placement (AP) biology exam from the College Board (2013) and the 2009 National Assessment of Educational Progress (NAEP) Interactive Computer and Hands-On Tasks Science Assessment (NCES 2012).

Most assessments at the state level test the STEM disciplines separately, although they may include performance tasks that assess science or math in the context of an applied design problem. For instance, a released science item from the 2009 Connecticut Academic Performance Test involves hands-on investigation of the effects of enzymes on the production of juice from applesauce or pears (CSDE 2009). Responses are rated on the credibility of the design of the investigation and interpretation of the data, measuring only scientific investigation practices. Another performance assessment asks students to conduct an experiment to determine the most durable material for a public sculpture. Scientific concepts and practices are the intended targets, and the evidence weighed aligns with scientific inquiry standards rather than standards for engineering design.

The Use of Information and Computer Technology in Assessment

Thanks to the rapidly advancing capabilities of digital and networking technologies, assessment functions related to authoring, delivering, collecting, and reporting measures of learning are becoming more efficient and economical. Technologies can expand the range of outcomes tested and support designs

Question 13: Nuclear Power Plant

In the nuclear power plant simulation below, the number of nuclear interactions produced by the reactor is regulated by the **Control Rods**. The power output is regulated by the **Generator Valve**. The **Control Rods** and the **Generator Valve** can be controlled by dragging the sliders up and down.

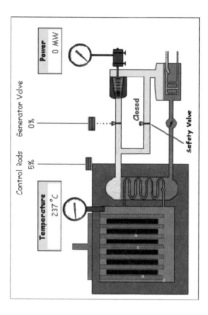

Set the generator valve at 80%. How far (%) should the control rods be lifted for the power plant to supply a continuous output of 800 Megawatts (MW) without the safety valve opening?

○ 55%.

○ 70%.

○ 85%.

○ 100%.

FIGURE 5-1 Interactive science item from the *Framework for NAEP Technology and Engineering Literacy* (TEL). Source: OECD 2010. Reprinted with permission.

of innovative tasks that can be used to assess progressions in integrated STEM learning (Quellmalz et al. 2012) or allow portfolio-based assessment of STEM practices, such as engineering design (Abts et al. 2013). Technology can also help align learning and assessment targets in an integrated STEM program with STEM standards and with embedded formative assessment items and summative tests.[2] Box 5-1 describes strategies for applying digital and networking technologies to support assessments of integrated STEM instruction.

EDUCATOR EXPERTISE

The expertise of educators, whether in classrooms or in after-/out-of-school settings, is a key factor—some would say *the* key factor—in determining whether the integration of STEM can be done well. At the most basic level, educator expertise combines knowledge of the subject matter with an understanding of effective approaches for teaching it to students with diverse learning styles. Such approaches include not only teaching strategies but also the skill with which educators plan lessons and work collaboratively to support student learning. Teachers' subject-matter knowledge is directly correlated with students' learning (e.g., Hill et al. 2005).

Because integrated STEM education is a relatively recent phenomenon, little is known from research about how best to support the development of educator expertise in this domain specifically. However, much that is known about the successful preparation of educators and about professional development generally is likely to be relevant to integrated STEM education. Research on K–12 STEM educators' expertise can provide insight into challenges and opportunities for preparing them to teach integrated STEM.

The following sections present a synthesis of research on three factors of particular relevance to the implementation of integrated STEM instruction: teachers' content knowledge, self-efficacy, and opportunities for collaboration. Where possible, we refer to research or cite examples from studies that tie directly to integrated STEM education. Preparing effective, confident teachers in single academic subjects is no easy task, and the task is likely to

---

[2] Embedded assessment attempts to measure knowledge or skill as part of the learning activity rather than as a separate step (i.e., test) after the fact. Formative assessment is typically employed by educators during the learning process to inform changes in instruction that will improve student understanding. Formative assessment typically involves qualitative feedback, rather than scores. Summative assessment (e.g., an end-of-unit exam) seeks to monitor educational outcomes, often for purposes of external accountability.

BOX 5-1
Possible Strategies for Leveraging Technology
to Assess Integrated STEM Learning

The high school course *Engineering the Future* (http://legacy.mos.org/
etf/) by the Museum of Science, Boston, engages students in four 8-week
projects on concepts of energy. Problems include how to use insulation
to create an energy-efficient building by minimizing loss of thermal energy and how to design a boat engine based on understanding of energy
transferred through pneumatic and hydraulic systems. Readings from
first-person narratives by engineers and technicians provide background
on how to apply engineering standards. The readings are keyed to sections in an engineer's notebook, in which students record their drawings,
design briefs, scale models, and prototypes. Math and science concepts
are brought in as prototypes are tested.

The engineer's notebook permits embedded formative assessment of
students' learning of engineering design, technology, science, and math
as they work through phases of the problems.Rubrics, or criteria, for evaluating paper-based entries (e.g., design briefs, sketches of prototypes,
worked calculations) provide evidence of progress and of outcomes need-
ing feedback and additional scaffolding to guide improvement. Rubrics
may be used by students, teachers, and/or external experts. Progress
reports on integrated STEM concepts and practices can be entered into
the notebooks and in a teacher class-level assessment record.

A digital version of the engineer's notebook could deliver questions
and problems designed to test the engineering design, science, math,

---

be more challenging for educators capable of guiding students in integrated
STEM education.

Teachers' STEM Content Knowledge

The prospects for widespread implementation of integrated STEM in and
out of the classroom may be limited by educators' STEM content knowledge.
While there is no universal measure of such knowledge, all indications are
that a significant percentage of educators have inadequate STEM content
knowledge in the individual STEM fields that they teach.

One important indicator of content knowledge is an undergraduate
degree in the subject being taught, but a significant proportion of elementary

and technology knowledge and practices involved during the phases of the project. These questions and problems could include text, graphics, photos and videos of sample designs, calculations, and prototype sketches. Some of the newly designed embedded assessment tasks and items could be automatically scored; some designs and drawings could be displayed for peer review and assessment. For the auto-scored tasks and items, the system could provide individualized feedback and scaffolding related to problematic concepts and practices, and generate progress reports.

The summative assessment tools are print self-evaluations, concept maps,[a] and end-of-project tests that can be administered electronically, with automatic scoring and rubric-based ratings generated for student and teacher analysis.

An alignment table could show the links between the intended learning targets and the different forms of evidence from the concept maps and end-of-project tests. The table would also document the extent to which learning targets for the distinct STEM disciplinary concepts and practices were at the same or different grade levels. A more ambitious summative assessment effort could develop brief simulation tasks for each unit to test whether students correctly apply the STEM concepts and practices to other integrated STEM design problems about energy concepts related to insulation and engines.

---

[a] Concept maps show relationships among different concepts and are a way to organize and structure knowledge.

teachers of science and mathematics are deficient by this measure. According to the 2012 National Survey of Science and Math Education (NSSME; Horizon Research 2013), just 5 percent of elementary teachers had a degree in science or science education, and 4 percent had a mathematics or mathematics education degree. Among middle school science teachers, 41 percent reported having earned a degree in science or science education, and 35 percent of middle school mathematics teachers had a degree in mathematics or mathematics education. The comparable figures for high school teachers were 82 and 73 percent for science and mathematics, respectively.

Some science and mathematics teachers without degrees obtain certification to teach those subjects, and this provides a proxy for content knowledge. For example, data from the 2007–2008 school year indicate that 12 and 16 percent of high school science and mathematics teachers, respectively, without a college degree in their subject received state certification to teach those subjects (NCES 2010).

Beyond majors and certifications, the professional associations representing K–12 science and mathematics teachers have proposed specific course-background standards for elementary and secondary educators. According to NSSME, the National Science Teachers Association (NSTA) recommends that elementary teachers take coursework in each of three areas: life, Earth, and physical sciences. Among elementary teachers, 74 percent have taken courses in at least two of the three recommended areas, NSSME found, and 73 percent of middle school general science teachers had taken courses in at least three of the four NSTA-recommended areas: life and Earth sciences, physics, and chemistry. The National Council of Teachers of Mathematics (NCTM) suggests coursework in five areas for elementary teachers: number and operations, algebra, geometry, probability, and statistics. NSSME found that 10 percent of elementary teachers met this standard, 42 percent of mathematics teachers at the secondary level took coursework in at least three of the areas, and 49 percent of middle school mathematics teachers took courses in all or five of the six areas recommended by NCTM. Guidance for the mathematical education of teachers is also offered by the Conference Board of the Mathematical Sciences (CBMS 2012).

Although they are in the majority by a wide margin, science and mathematics teachers are not the only teachers of K–12 STEM. Some 45 undergraduate programs in the United States prepare technology teachers (CTETE 2012), most of whom will be working in middle and high schools.[3] The technology teacher education curriculum includes mathematics and science coursework, though specific requirements vary. A survey of technology teacher preparation programs (McAlister 2004) found that most required between 2 and 8 credits of mathematics and 6 to 8 credits of science. The curriculum also includes coursework in specific areas of technology—such as communications, manufacturing, transportation, construction, and medicine and health—and on the relationship between technology and society. The basis for most programs' curricula is *Standards for Technological Literacy: Content for the Study of Technology* (ITEEA 2000). With the exception of teachers licensed under emergency certification programs, states require technology teachers to have a bachelor's degree in technology education or in industrial arts.

---

[3] Technology education is discussed in Chapter 1.

Over the last decade, technology educators have begun to teach aspects of engineering, and engineering coursework is now offered by some teacher education programs (Fantz and Katsioloudis 2011). Courses such as engineering math and statistics include mathematics and science content; others address engineering design as well as more narrow subjects, such as thermodynamics and mechatronics.

Educator Self-Efficacy

A teacher's self-efficacy depends on adequate background in the STEM subject(s) being taught, the ability to effectively transfer that knowledge and understanding to students—what is called pedagogical content knowledge (Shulman 1987)—and confidence in both areas. Self-efficacy, research shows, is a major determinant of teacher effectiveness (e.g., Berman and McLauglin 1977; Gibson and Dembo 1984; Woolfolk Hoy and Davis 2005).

Not surprisingly, educators who are or feel deficient in their content knowledge are less likely to believe they can teach the material effectively (Peterson et al. 1989; Rubek and Enochs 1991). The literature reports abundant data showing that many teachers are reluctant to teach science (Wenner 1993) and to a lesser extent mathematics, especially in the elementary and middle grades. Several studies suggest that efficacy is a significant factor contributing to this reluctance (Baker 1991; Riggs and Enochs 1990; Wenner 2001).

Lack of confidence in mathematics and science knowledge (Diefes-Dux and Duncan 2007) and fear of engineering (Cunningham 2007) have been tied to educator reluctance to engage in professional development related to engineering. The NSSME (Horizon Research 2013) found that only 4 percent of elementary teachers[4] and only 6 and 7 percent of middle and high school science teachers, respectively, felt very well prepared to teach about engineering. By comparison, 39 percent and 77 percent of elementary teachers reported that they felt very well prepared to teach science and mathematics, respectively. Depending on the specific topic,[5] between 5 and 58 percent of

---

[4] The survey defined engineering broadly as "nature of engineering and technology, design processes, analyzing and improving technological systems, interactions between technology and society."

[5] Teachers rated their confidence in teaching 19 specific topics across earth/space science, biology/life science, chemistry, and physics. The lowest level of confidence by far for both middle and high school teachers was in "modern physics (e.g., special relativity)."

middle school teachers and 19 and 83 percent of high school teachers felt very well prepared to teach science. For mathematics topics,[6] high confidence ranged from 48 to 88 percent for middle school teachers and from 30 to 90 percent of high school teachers.

In a specific illustration of the problem, William Hunter of Illinois State University told the committee about the development and implementation of the iMaST (Integrated Mathematics, Science, and Technology) curriculum.[7] It includes 195 learning cycles, 107 readings, and 16 thematic modules that have been tested and revised for grades 6 through 8, but most teachers have been reluctant to fully implement the program, he reported. Math teachers were especially hesitant because of their lack of confidence in teaching science.

It is highly likely that educator self-efficacy will play a critical role in effective integrated STEM education (e.g., Koirala and Bowman 2003). Research is needed to determine how best to address the challenge of inadequate self-efficacy among teachers of integrated STEM, but, as described in the next section, some programs are available for enhancing teacher's STEM content knowledge, which may contribute to self-efficacy.

Developing Expertise for Teaching Integrated STEM

Because integrated STEM education must address at least two of the four disciplines, one basic question is to what extent a teacher must be responsible for (have expertise in) multiple STEM content areas. As we note above, even in the individual STEM subjects, K–12 teacher expertise is often lower than what professional organizations in the field recommend. It is therefore important to determine ways to help K–12 educators develop substantive understanding of more than one STEM field.

Although expertise related to the individual subjects is important for integrated STEM, content knowledge alone is not sufficient. Teachers also need to know about and become expert in pedagogical strategies that support students in integrated experiences. For example, as discussed in Chapters 3 and 4, teachers need to know how to provide instructional supports that help students recognize connections between disciplines. They also need to

---

[6] Teachers rated their confidence in teaching algebraic thinking, the number system and operations, functions, measurement, geometry, modeling, statistics and probability, and discrete mathematics. The lowest level of confidence for both middle and high school teachers was in discrete mathematics.

[7] For more information: http://cemast.illinoisstate.edu/downloads/imast/glance2011.doc.

be able to assist students in developing proficiency in individual subjects in ways that complement and support students' learning in integrated activities.

Examples of Preservice Teacher Preparation in Integrated STEM

A small number of teacher education programs around the country are making efforts to prepare prospective or current K–12 teachers with appropriate content knowledge in more than one STEM subject. One of them is UTeach*Engineering* (www.uteachengineering.org/), at the University of Texas at Austin (UT), a collaboration among UT's Cockrell School of Engineering, its Colleges of Natural Sciences and Education, and the Austin Independent School District.

UTeach*Engineering* is modeled after the UTeach Natural Sciences program (www.uteach.utexas.edu/), which encourages undergraduate STEM majors to pursue careers in secondary-level mathematics and science teaching. UTeach*Engineering* provides a broad content foundation in STEM for physics, mathematics, chemistry, and engineering majors to teach grades 8–12 under a new Texas Education Agency certification, 174 Mathematics/ Physical Science/Engineering 8–12 (TEA 2011). Students seeking this certification who are majoring in physics, chemistry, or mathematics must supplement core content coursework in their major with upper-division classes in the other two subjects (e.g., a mathematics major must add coursework in chemistry and physics) and successfully complete three upper-division engineering classes that teach fundamentals in the context of design problems. Engineering students seeking the same certification must fulfill all of their engineering degree requirements and complete additional content coursework in chemistry, physics, and mathematics (e.g., structure of modern geometry; foundations, functions, and regression models). All students in the UTeach program, regardless of their major, complete professional development coursework and a teaching apprenticeship.

The 174 certification is relatively new; UT Austin was approved to offer it beginning in 2012. To date, four UTeach*Engineering* graduates—three in physics and one in engineering—have earned the certification, and at least seven students in physics, chemistry, and mathematics are pursuing it, as are some of the 37 engineering majors enrolled in UTeach courses (Cheryl Farmer, UTeach*Engineering*, personal communication, March 1, 2013).

Nearly half of the other 32 institutions around the country involved in UTeach Natural Sciences replication programs are enrolling engineering students: at the University of Massachusetts, Lowell, 16 of 71 UTeach students are engineering majors; at the University of Kansas, 21 of 307 students are engineering majors; and at Southern Polytechnic State University, 5 of 29 are engineering majors. In spring 2013, the University of Colorado, Boulder, announced creation of CU Teach Engineering, which will offer general engineering majors the opportunity to earn a license to teach secondary science or mathematics (UCB 2013). Similar programs are being implemented at the University of Tennessee, Chattanooga, and the University of California, Berkeley.

Colorado State University (CSU) requires additional coursework of engineering science majors that allows them to obtain teaching certificates in technology education. The program, a collaboration between the university's schools of engineering and education, has enrolled 35 students so far and graduated 12, all with primary licenses in technology education and additional endorsements in mathematics. More than half of the program's graduates are women (Michael DeMiranda, CSU, personal communication, February 27, 2013). The MST (math, science, technology) elementary education degree offered by The College of New Jersey (TCNJ; O'Brien 2010) and described in Box 2-7 in Chapter 2, requires students to take coursework across multiple STEM areas. And Boise State University's (BSU) master of science in STEM education program for in-service teachers requires 33 credit hours, including 14 hours of STEM content courses and a 3-credit course covering fundamentals of education research.

A program at Purdue University educates future secondary school math and science teachers, engineering education doctoral students, and students in a graduate-level engineering course designed to provide strategies for integrating engineering in stand-alone or integrated environments (Carr and Strobel 2011). The program uses a combination of face-to-face and online instruction that models a project-based learning approach, and there are opportunities for students to apply research-based methods of integration and engineering instruction throughout the learning process. Course outcomes, including understanding of concepts, knowledge, and attitudes are assessed using student products, concept maps, and student feedback.

At the National Center for Elementary STEM Education based at St. Catherine University in Minnesota, all elementary education majors obtain a STEM certificate that requires three cross-disciplinary, inquiry-based courses: Chemistry of Life, Environmental Biology, and Makin' and Breakin': Engineering in Your World. There have been 76 graduates of the program since 2010 (Patricia Born Selly, National Center for STEM Elementary Education, personal communication, November 8, 2013). The university also offers a 15-credit graduate STEM certificate program for in-service elementary teachers. The program, which initially served only Montessori teachers but now enrolls teachers from non-Montesorri schools, pairs in-depth, hands-on learning for one week each summer with online mentoring and support during the academic year. The graduate program, which since 2009 has awarded 227 certificates, is driven in part by the state's K–12 science standards, which include learning goals related to the practice of engineering (MDE 2009).Virginia Tech (VT) has taken a different tack with its Integrative STEM Education Graduate Program (www.soe.vt.edu/istemed/). Its goal is to prepare STEM teachers and administrators to design, implement, and investigate integrative approaches to STEM education (Mark Sanders, Virginia Tech, personal communication, February 22, 2013). The program, begun in 2005, currently enrolls about 50 students pursuing master's, EdS, EdD, or PhD degrees. Most earn a 12-semester Integrative STEM Education Graduate Certificate on the way to completing their degree. More than half of the students are middle/high school science, mathematics, and/or elementary school teachers, or K–12 administrators; the rest are full-time technology or engineering teachers, coordinators, or administrators. Courses are taught on campus, but because most enrolled students are working full-time off campus, interactive video-based class sessions are also conducted in real time via the Web.

Students in the VT program can take advantage of a 2,800-square-foot STEM Education Collaboratory, a laboratory and classroom space for investigating, assessing, and promoting innovative design-based approaches to teaching and learning (Wells 2013). In fall 2011, for example, the collaboratory hosted a professional development session for elementary master teachers from around the country who planned to teach the technology, engineering, environment, mathematics, and science (TEEMS) curriculum developed by Engineering by Design™ (www.iteea.org/EbD/ebd.htm), a program of the International Technology and Engineering Educators Association.

The UT, CSU, TCNJ, BSU, Purdue, and St. Catherine programs indicate that it is possible to enhance the STEM content knowledge of both new and experienced teachers. But it is less clear, because there is virtually no research on the topic, that this additional knowledge is put to use in the classroom or in ways that support students' ability to make connections between or among concepts and practices in more than one area of STEM. In this regard, the VT program's goal of supporting teacher and administrator efforts to carry out "integrative" STEM education appears unique. But it, too, lacks empirical study of the impact of teacher certification on student learning.

Having the content knowledge and pedagogical skills to teach STEM in an integrated fashion is only part of the challenge of implementation, however. Even educators who graduate from one of the programs described above will have relatively few options in terms of schools that are equipped to support integrated approaches to STEM education. It is the committee's sense that, at this time, most educators with broad STEM backgrounds are likely to find themselves teaching single subjects in fairly traditional settings.

Examples of Professional Development for In-Service Integrated STEM Teachers

Professional development can boost the STEM content knowledge of in-service teachers, as teachers with expertise in one area, such as science education, pursue coursework to build knowledge in another area, such as mathematics. While such programs vary in structure and content, research on professional development has found that effectiveness increases significantly if teachers are engaged over extended periods—a week or more—and have access to ongoing support and mentoring beyond the formal training.

A basic premise of many professional development programs reviewed by the committee is that if teachers have not themselves experienced integration of science, mathematics, technology, and/or engineering, they are not likely to teach integrated curricula for these subjects in their classrooms. In short, teachers need an understanding of and experience with integrated STEM if they are to teach in an integrated manner.

In one fairly representative study, Basista and Mathews (2002) describe a small-scale (22 teachers of grades 4–12) university-based professional development program on integrating mathematics and science. The program consisted of an intensive summer institute followed by academic-year support activities and visits to participating teachers' classrooms. The authors report that a minimum duration of 3 weeks (contact time of 72 hours) was necessary to bring about significant shifts in teachers' beliefs, pedagogical preparation, and subject content knowledge. Institute courses were team taught by science and mathematics educators, and teachers were "immersed" in inquiry-based learning environments where they worked on integrated science and mathematics units in cooperative groups of three or four. Program assessment, based on before and after evaluations, found that teachers' content knowledge, pedagogical knowledge, and confidence increased. However, because the design did not include a control or comparison group, it is not possible to attribute the results to the program alone, nor are the results generalizable. Nevertheless, the findings suggest that this approach has the potential to make a positive contribution to preparing teachers for effective integrated STEM instruction.

Daugherty (2009) examined five integrated STEM programs (Engineering the Future–Project Lead the Way, Mathematics Across the Middle School, MST Curriculum Project, the Infinity Project, and INSPIRES) that provide professional development for in-service teachers. Participating teachers agreed on three aspects that contributed to the programs' effectiveness: (1) hands-on activities, (2) teacher collaboration, and (3) instructor credibility. Given the multiple ways engineering may be portrayed in the classroom, Daugherty suggests that more research is needed to better understand how teachers and students best learn engineering in order to design effective professional development.

A number of K–12 engineering curricula include professional development that familiarizes in-service teachers in technology, science, and mathematics with the engineering design process (NAE and NRC 2009). For example, a 2012 survey of teachers participating in training to teach Project Lead the Way (PLTW; www.pltw.org), one of the largest engineering-focused curriculum projects in the country, found that 32 percent were certified to teach science, 30 percent were certified to teach technology education, and 13 percent were certified to teach mathematics[8] (Anne Jones, PLTW, personal communication, March 12, 2013).

Collaboration

Research findings indicate that teacher collaboration and the development of professional learning communities (PLC; Box 5-2) will be important to effective integrated STEM education. Such relationships not only support the development and revision of integrated curriculum and instruction but also nurture communities of practice that may extend beyond the classroom or after-/out-of-school setting. Online tools, particularly the Internet, have the potential to facilitate development of PLCs and to support professional development more generally (NRC 2007).

---

[8] These numbers do not add to 100 percent because some teachers reported certifications in two or all three of the areas of science, technology, and mathematics, and these respondents are not reported here. In addition, 9 percent of teachers indicated that they had a certification in an area other than these three subjects.

BOX 5-2
Professional Learning Communities

Professional learning communities (PLCs) provide opportunities for teachers to pursue ongoing learning and professional growth, which research suggests are tied to teacher self-efficacy and effectiveness. DuFour (2004, p.9) characterizes PLCs as "a systematic process in which teachers work together to analyze and improve their classroom practice. Teachers work in teams, engaging in an ongoing cycle of questions that promote deep team learning. This process, in turn, leads to higher levels of student achievement."

For example, when the Martha and Josh Morriss Mathematics and Engineering Elementary School was established in 2007, the Texarkana Intermediate School District introduced a teacher professional development curriculum that provided math content but also empowered teachers to engage in ongoing curriculum design and revision through opportunities for collaboration. In a presentation to the committee, Principal Rick Sandlin and Curriculum Coordinator Rona Jameson noted that elementary school teachers' lack of confidence and competence in math and science limited their ability to effectively and meaningfully integrate the STEM disciplines. All teachers were therefore required to complete a master's degree in curriculum and instruction, available through a program created in partnership with the local university. In the summer of 2007, teachers took two courses—Interdisciplinary Curriculum Development and Interdisciplinary Curriculum Delivery—intended to build teamwork and skill in collaborative design and delivery of integrated STEM curriculum units, with support as needed from the principal and the university-based curriculum coach. The Morriss school efforts, reported in a case study by Hunter (2009), have since been adapted in a districtwide curriculum review process that incorporates curriculum and instruction self-evaluation.

An analysis of nine midwestern schools and districts that implement the PLTW curriculum identified teacher collaboration as a key element in developing a "STEM culture" (Meeder 2012). At Thomas Worthington High School in suburban Columbus, Ohio, PLTW teachers and their colleagues in mathematics and science formed a STEM Collaborative Team for lesson planning. Using a curriculum mapping process, the team identified topics taught across disciplines but delivered at different points in the year and thus coordinated instruction among courses. A mathematics teacher quoted in the Meeder analysis said, "Teaching STEM math has taken lots of extra work to develop the lessons. But the payoff is great. . . . Working with other teachers makes me a better teacher."

At Manor (Texas) New Technology High School, all teachers participate in at least 150 hours of professional development yearly (E3 Alliance 2009). This includes specialized training with New Tech's project-based-learning school model, in which administrators also participate, and training provided by Texas Tech University to implement engineering across the curriculum. Each Monday morning at Manor begins with a two-hour "teacher school," in which teachers introduce or critique projects, analyze data, and learn about each other's instructional strategies that have proven effective. By one account, this two-hour period of professional development is critical to the school's success (ICLE 2010). Although there is a shared library of lessons, rubrics, and course material from the New Tech Foundation, Manor teachers are actively engaged in creating their own project-based lessons and learning activities. Many of the school's teachers participate in the national Teacher Advancement Program (www.tapsystem.org), qualifying them to pursue other positions such as career counselor, mentor, or master teacher.

Aimee Kennedy, principal of Metro Early College High School in Columbus, Ohio, told the committee that teacher education and professional development are critical to her school's efforts to integrate the STEM subjects. Ohio State University (OSU) and Battelle Industries jointly established the school, and it serves as a research and development site for the OSU College of Education and Human Ecology, "to fundamentally change how teacher and leadership preparation occurs" (Metro fact sheet, n.d.). School leadership priorities for teachers include strong content knowledge, "instructional agility," and a professional culture that pushes practice (North 2011); Kennedy reported that, in 2010–2011, the focus of professional development was on "design challenges."

OTHER CONTEXTUAL FACTORS

Although standards, assessment, and educator expertise must be attended to in implementing integrated STEM, the larger context of the school or after-/out-of-school entity—its policies, norms, practices, and administrative leadership—is also important. Schools are influenced by the norms, practices, and policies of the school district, and both schools and after-/

out-of-school learning programs are affected by parents, taxpayers, higher education, and business leaders in the community. The community and school district, in turn, are influenced by norms, practices, and policies at the state, regional, and federal levels. To understand how these different factors may encourage or discourage effective implementation of integrated STEM experiences, it helps to view the education enterprise as a complex system with interacting parts (e.g., Confrey and Maloney 2011).

A detailed discussion of all aspects of the education system that might constrain or advance integrated STEM education is beyond the scope of this report, but recent studies of STEM education in general shed light on the topic. The NRC (2011a) report *Successful K–12 STEM Education: Identifying Effective Approaches in Science, Technology, Engineering, and Mathematics* identified elements shared by schools that showed improvements in student learning in mathematics and science (see Box 5-3). And it suggests that districts provide instructional leaders with professional development that helps them create conditions favorable for students' success in STEM. Similarly,

---

BOX 5-3
Elements of School Culture That Support STEM Learning

1. School leadership as the driver for change. Principals must be strategic, focused on instruction, and inclusive of others in the leadership work.
2. Professional capacity or the quality of the faculty and staff recruited to the school, their beliefs and values about changes, the quality of ongoing professional development, and the capacity of staff to work together.
3. Parent-community ties that involve active outreach to make school a welcoming place for parents, engage them in supporting their children's academic success, and strengthen connections to other local institutions.
4. A student-centered learning climate that is safe, welcoming, stimulating, and nurturing for all students.
5. Instructional guidance focused on the organization of the curriculum, the nature of academic demands or challenges it poses, and the tools teachers have to advance learning (such as instructional materials).

SOURCE: NRC (2011a).

administrators and other leaders in schools or districts that seek to develop integrated STEM programs will need to understand integrated STEM education and strategies they can use to ensure its success.

Although the project's data gathering did not focus on this dimension of K–12 education, information and communications technology (ICT) is playing an increasingly important role in delivering content, connecting students and teachers, and monitoring learning and other outcomes. Certain types of ICT, such as games and simulations, show promise for supporting student conceptual understanding and motivating interest (NRC 2011b). But overall, evidence regarding improved learning outcomes from blended and online learning approaches is thin (Means et al. 2013), suggesting the need for continuing research on the effective use of these tools for both students and educators.

CONCLUSIONS

State adoption and implementation of the CCSSM and NGSS will require a deeper understanding of how to create effective integrated STEM experiences that engage students in the practices of mathematics, science, and engineering while applying disciplinary content knowledge. If done well, the implementation should lead to fundamental shifts in the teaching of STEM in schools as the standards make explicit the connections between science, mathematics, and engineering and provide a framework for schools and informal education programs to integrate STEM education.

Implementation of integrated STEM experiences in school and in after-/out-of-school settings will in many cases demand educator expertise beyond that needed to teach any of the STEM subjects individually. Thus, many educators will need additional content and pedagogical content knowledge in disciplinary areas beyond their previous education or experience. Such supplementation will require time, money, planning, and monitoring for effectiveness.

We learned of several programs that provide preservice opportunities to develop educators with deep knowledge in more than one STEM field. But the number of teachers participating in these initiatives is still quite small, and we know little about the extent to which they are teaching in ways that might be considered integrated. For teachers already in the classroom, a number of curriculum projects include professional development to build content knowledge in more than one STEM discipline. Little is known, however, about how or whether these efforts address teacher expertise related to integrated STEM education.

Evidence does indicate that educators need opportunities and training to work collaboratively to deliver effective, integrated STEM instruction. Collaboration should involve staff in the school (e.g., joint lesson planning among STEM teachers) but may extend beyond the classroom to include STEM and education faculty in postsecondary institutions, educators in after-/out-of-school settings, and STEM professionals in industry.

As noted, the recently published NGSS emphasize the role of engineering design in facilitating student learning of scientific concepts. Given current low levels of confidence among K–12 educators in the teaching of engineering (Horizon Research 2013), it may be especially important for both new and experienced science teachers to become familiar with the engineering design process and how it can be integrated into science teaching.

The quest for integrated STEM programs that engage students in real-world applications of STEM knowledge and practices will require significantly different assessments of learning. To understand the strengths and weaknesses of current assessment practices, analyses need to be conducted of integrated STEM programs and of formative and summative STEM assessments. Analyses of integrated STEM programs may reveal additional opportunities for assessment. Promising exemplars of integrated STEM assessment of individual and team learning could be identified and evaluated. Pilot studies of assessment designs could contribute to the development of next-generation integrated STEM assessments, which are to provide evidence supporting the promise and claimed benefits of integrated STEM teaching and learning.

REFERENCES

Abts, L., E. Ball, and R. Reshetar. 2013. Portfolio and rubrics for assessing STEM learning. Paper accepted for presentation at the AP Annual Conference, Las Vegas, Nevada, July 2013.

AERA (American Educational Research Association), APA (American Psychological Association), and NCME (National Council on Measurement in Education). 1999. Standards for Psychological Testing. Washington: American Educational Research Association.

Baker, D.R. 1991. A summary of research in science education—1998. Science Education 75:1–35.

Basista, B., and S. Mathews. 2002. Integrated science and mathematics professional development programs. School Science and Mathematics 102(7):359–370.

Berman, P., M.W. McLaughlin, G.V. Bass-Golod, E. Pauly, and G.L. Zellman. 1997. Federal Programs Supporting Education Change. Vol. 7 Factors Affecting Implementation and Continuation. Report R-1589/7-HEW. Santa Monica, CA: RAND Corp.

Carr, R.L., and J. Strobel. 2011, April. Integrating engineering into secondary math and science curriculum: A course for preparing teachers. IEEE 1st Integrated STEM Education Conference, Ewing, NJ.

CBMS (Conference Board of the Mathematical Sciences). 2012. The mathematical education of teachers II. Available at http://cbmsweb.org/MET2/index.htm (retrieved July 18, 2013).

College Board. 2013. AP Biology—Course and Exam Description. Effective Fall 2012. Revised Edition. Available at http://media.collegeboard.com/digitalServices/pdf/ap/IN120084785_BiologyCED_Effective_Fall_2012_Revised_lkd.pdf (retrieved September 5, 2013).

Confrey, J., and A. Maloney. 2011. Engineering (for) effectiveness in mathematics education. Intervention at the instructional core in an era of common core standards. Paper presented for the workshop of the Committee on Highly Successful Schools or Programs for K-12 STEM Education. National Research Council, Washington, DC, May 10–12, 2011.

Crismond, D. 2001. Learning and using science ideas when doing investigate-and-redesign tasks. A study of naïve, novice, and expert designers doing constrained and scaffolded design work. Journal of Research in Science Teaching 38(7):791–820.

CSDE (Connecticut State Department of Education). 2009. "Enzyme Investigation." CAPT Science 2009 Administration. Released Items and Scored Student Responses. Available at www.csde.state.ct.us/public/cedar/assessment/capt/resources/released_items/2009/ReleaseItems_state_082709.pdf (retrieved September 5, 2013).

CTETE (Council on Technology and Engineering Teacher Education). 2012. Technology & Engineering Teacher Education Directory: Institutions, Degree Data, and Personnel. 2012–2013, 51st Edition. Available at http://media.wix.com/ugd/68f68f_5c157e30d8ded7fc2709c7b2f4d3e1df.pdf?dn=51%2BTETE%2BDirectory%2B2012–2013.pdf (retrieved February 21, 2013).

Daugherty, J. 2009. Engineering professional development design for secondary school teachers: A multiple case study. Journal of Technology Education 21(1):10–24.

Davidson, M., H. Evens, and R. McCormick. 1998. Bridging the gap: The use of concepts from science and mathematics in design and technology at KS 3. Available at https://dspace.lboro.ac.uk/dspace-jspui/bitstream/2134/1419/1/davidson98.pdf (retrieved November 15, 2013).

Diefes-Dux, H., and D. Duncan. 2007. Adapting Engineering is Elementary professional development to encourage open-ended mathematical modeling. Paper presented to the Committee on K–12 Engineering Education, National Academy of Engineering and National Research Council, Workshop and Third Meeting, Washington, DC, October 22, 2007.

DuFour, R. 2004. What is a "professional learning community?" Available at www.allthingsplc.info/pdf/articles/DuFourWhatIsAProfessionalLearningCommunity.pdf (retrieved September 5, 2013).

E3 Alliance. 2009. Case study of New Manor High School: Promising practices for comprehensive high schools. Available at http://mnths.manorisd.net/ourpages/auto/2012/3/7/39399794/MNTHS_Case%20Study.pdf (retrieved July 17, 2013).

Fantz, T.D., and P.J. Katsioloudis. 2011. Analysis of engineering content within technology education programs. Journal of Technology Education 23(1): 19–31. Available at http://scholar.lib.vt.edu/ejournals/JTE/v23n1/pdf/fantz.pdf (retrieved February 15, 2013).

Gibson, S., and M. Dembo. 1984. Teacher efficacy: A construct validation. Journal of Educational Psychology 76(4):569–582.

Hartzler, D.S. 2000. A meta-analysis of studies conducted on integrated curriculum programs and their effects on student achievement. Unpublished dissertation. Indiana University, Bloomington, IN.

Hill, H.C., B. Rowan, and D.L. Ball. 2005. Effects of teachers' mathematical knowledge for teaching on student achievement. American Educational Research Journal 42(2):371–406.

Horizon Research. 2013. Report of the National Survey of Science and Mathematics Education. February 2013. Available at www.horizon-research.com/2012nssme/wp-content/uploads/2013/02/2012-NSSME-Full-Report1.pdf (retrieved February 27, 2013).

Hunter, M.S. 2009. Morriss Math and Engineering Elementary School: A Case Study of K–5 STEM Education Program Development. Columbus, OH: The Past Foundation.

ICLE (International Center for Leadership in Education). 2010. Manor New Technology High School. Available at www.leadered.com/msc11/handouts/casestudies/49Manor%20New%20Tech%20HS%20Profile.pdf (retrieved July 17, 2013).

ITEEA (International Technology and Engineering Educators Association). 2000. Standards for Technological Literacy: Content for the Study of Technology. Available at www.iteea.org/TAA/PDFs/xstnd.pdf (retrieved September 5, 2013).

Koirala, H.P., and J.K. Bowman. 2003. Preparing middle level preservice treachers to integrated mathematics and science: Problems and possibilities. School Science and Mathematics 103(3):145–154.

McAlister, B.K. 2004, November 5. Are technology education teachers prepared to teach engineering design and analytical methods? Paper presented to the 91st Mississippi Valley Technology Teacher Education Conference, Chicago, IL. Unpublished.

MDE (Minnesota Department of Education). 2009. Minnesota Academic Standards—Science K-12 2009 Version. Available at http://stem.stkate.edu/pdf/mn_standards.pdf (retrieved November 15, 2013).

Means, B., Y. Toyama, R. Murphy, and M. Baki. 2013. The effectiveness of online and blended learning: A Meta-analysis of the empirical literature. Teachers College Record 115(3):1–47.

Meeder, H. 2012. Strategies to develop a school-wide STEM culture. Presentation to the National Academy of Engineering and National Research Council Committee on Integrated STEM Education. July 12, 2012, Washington, DC. Slides available at www.nae.edu/File.aspx?id=61600 (retrieved July 17, 2013).

NAGB (National Assessment Governing Board). 2010. Technology and Engineering Literacy Framework for the 2014 National Assessment of Educational Progress—Pre-Publication Edition. Available at www.nagb.org/content/nagb/assets/documents/publications/frameworks/prepub_naep_tel_framework_2014.pdf (retrieved September 5, 2013).

NAE (National Academy of Engineering) and NRC (National Research Council). 2009. Engineering in K-12 education: Understanding the status and improving the prospects. Available at www.nap.edu/catalog.php?record_id=12635 (retrieved September 6, 2013).

NCES (National Center for Education Statistics). 2010. Status and trends in the education of racial and ethnic groups (NCES 2010–015). Washington, DC. Available at www.air.org/files/AIR-NCESracial_stats__trends1.pdf (retrieved August 22, 2013).

NCES. 2012. The Nation's Report Card: Science in Action: Hands-on and interactive computer tasks from the 2009 Science Assessment (NCES 2012–468). Washington, DC.

NGACPB (National Governors Association Center for Best Practices). 2010. Common Core State Standards for Mathematics. Available online at www.corestandards.org/assets/CCSSI_Math%20Standards.pdf (retrieved January 14, 2014).

North, C. 2011. Designing STEM pathways through early college: Ohio's Metro Early College High School. Available at www.themetroschool.org/assets/documents/ECDS_DesigningSTEMPathways_081511.pdf (retrieved August 22, 2013).

NRC. 2001. Knowing what students know: The science and design of educational assessment. Available at www.nap.edu/catalog.php?record_id=10019 (retrieved September 5, 2013).

NRC. 2005. Systems for state science assessment. Available at www.nap.edu/catalog.php?record_id=11312 (retrieved September 5, 2013).

NRC. 2007. Enhancing professional development for teachers: Potential uses of information technology. Report of a workshop. Committee on Enhancing Professional Development for Teachers, National Academies Teacher Advisory Council. Available online at www.nap.edu/catalog.php?record_id=11995 (retrieved November 19, 2013).

NRC. 2011a. Successful K–12 STEM education: Identifying effective approaches in science, technology, engineering, and mathematics. Available at www.nap.edu/catalog.php?record_id=13158 (retrieved September 6, 2013).

NRC. 2011b. Learning science through computer games and simulations. Available at www.nap.edu/catalog.php?record_id=13078 (retrieved November 18, 2013).

NRC. 2012. A framework for K–12 science education: Practices, crosscutting concepts, and core ideas. Available at www.nap.edu/catalog.php?record_id=13165 (retrieved September 5, 2013).

NRC. 2013a. Next Generation Science Standards: For states, by states. Available at www.nap.edu/NGSS/ (retrieved September 4, 2013).

NRC. 2013b. Developing Assessments for the Next Generation Science Standards. Committee on Asssessment of Science Proficiency in K-12. Available online at www.nap.edu/catalog.php?record_id=18409 (retrieved January 14, 2014).

O'Brien, S. 2010. Characterization of a unique undergraduate multidisciplinary STEM K-5 teacher preparation program. Journal of Technology Education 21(2). Available at http://scholar.lib.vt.edu/ejournals/JTE/v21n2/obrien.html (retrieved January 21, 2014).

OECD (Organisation for Economic Co-operation and Development), 2010. Figure 63, "Sample item showing bias towards female: Nuclear power plant," in PISA computer-based assessment of student skills in science. Paris: OECD Publishing.

Peterson, P., E. Fennema, T. Carpenter, and M. Loef. 1989. Teachers' pedagogical content beliefs in mathematics. Cognition and Instruction 6:1–40.

Quellmalz, E.S., M.J. Timms, B.C. Buckley, J. Davenport, M. Loveland, and M.D. Silberglitt. 2012. 21st century dynamic assessment. In M. Mayrath, J. Clarke-Midura, and D.H. Robinson (Eds.), Technology-based assessments for 21st century skills: Theoretical and practical implications from modern research. Charlotte, NC: Information Age Publishing.

Riggs, L., and L. Enochs. 1990. Toward the development of an elementary teacher's science teaching efficacy belief instrument. Science Education 74:625–637.

Rubeck, M.L., and L.G. Enochs. 1991. A path analytic model of variables that influence science and chemistry teaching self-efficacy and outcome expectancy in middle school science teachers. Paper presented at the annual meeting of the National Association for Research in Science Teaching, April, Lake Geneva, WI.

Shulman, L.S. 1987. Knowledge and teaching: Foundations of the new reform. Harvard Educational Review 57(1):1–22.

TEA (Texas Education Agency). 2011. Preparation Manual: 174 Mathematics/Physical Science/Engineering 8–12. Texas Examinations of Educator Standards. Princeton, NJ: ETS.

UCB (University of Colorado Boulder). 2013. CU-Boulder launches new degree to create STEM teachers through engineering. Press release. Available at www.colorado.edu/news/releases/2013/08/22/cu-boulder-launches-new-degree-create-stem-teachers-through-engineering (retrieved August 22, 2013).

Wells, J.G. 2013. Integrative STEM Education at Virginia Tech: Graduate preparation for tomorrow's leaders. Technology and Engineering Teacher 72(5):28–34.

Wenner, G. 1993. Relationship between science knowledge levels and belief toward science instruction held by pre-service elementary teachers. Journal of Science Education and Technology 2:461–468.

Wenner, G. 2001. Science and mathematics efficacy beliefs held by practicing and prospective teachers: A 5-year perspective. Journal of Science Education and Technology 10(2):181–187.

Woodfolk Hoy, A., and H. Davis. 2005 Teachers' sense of efficacy and adolescent achievement. In T. Urdan and F. Pajares (Eds.), Adolescence and Education: Vol. 5: Self-Efficacy Beliefs During Adolescence, pp. 117–137. Greenwich, CT: Information Age.

6

Findings, Recommendations, and Research Agenda

There is considerable concern among policymakers, educators, employers, and others about improving K–12 STEM education in the United States and in raising the number and quality of students who are both interested in and prepared to enter STEM and related professions. Historically, most efforts to improve STEM education at the precollege level have focused on the individual subjects—particularly science and mathematics—rather than on how or whether they can or should be connected in ways that might improve student thinking, learning, engagement, motivation, or persistence.

Several converging forces have elevated the importance of understanding the potential value—as well as the limitations and challenges—of integrated STEM education. One development is the small but growing presence of engineering in K–12 classrooms[1] and out-of-school settings. Because engineering by its nature draws on ideas and practices from the other three STEM disciplines, it is has been seen by some as a natural focus for integration efforts. The recent publication of the *Next Generation Science Standards*

---

[1] Two of the most widespread programs are Engineering is Elementary (EiE) and Project Lead the Way (PLTW). EiE estimates that its curriculum has reached 4.1 million students and has been used by 52,000 teachers (Christine Cunningham, Museum of Science, Boston, personal communication, August 1, 2013). PLTW estimates that 5,500 schools offer at least one of its programs each year, enrolling between 400,000 and 500,000 students annually (Jennifer Cahill, PLTW, personal communication, August 7, 2013).

135

(NGSS; Achieve 2013), which suggest that certain science concepts be learned in the context of engineering design, is a significant illustration of the belief that concepts and practices from different STEM disciplines can be learned in concert. This appealing but still somewhat intuitive notion, however, is not yet strongly supported by findings from research, as indicated by the committee's review of the literature.

A key driver of the NGSS was the desire to present science to students in ways that more closely represent how scientists experience it: as a practice requiring application of knowledge from multiple disciplines. This speaks to a second factor driving interest in integrated STEM education: concern about how to better prepare US students to enter the workplace, whether immediately after high school or following postsecondary coursework. An increasing share of jobs across a range of economic sectors, not just in science and engineering, is likely to require some background in the STEM subjects (Carnevale et al. 2011). In addition, employers have made clear their need for workers who can flexibly apply knowledge to solve practical problems (AACU 2013). Development of problem-solving expertise is neither the goal nor an assured outcome of every integrated STEM education initiative, but the committee's review of programs finds problem solving[2] to be a common element of many integrated approaches to STEM learning.

Finally, some of the impetus for integrated STEM education is undoubtedly driven by dissatisfaction with traditional approaches to science and mathematics education in the United States. Although decades of education reform have brought significant changes to curricula, standards, and professional development in these subjects, much science and mathematics teaching still emphasizes rote skills and memorization; relatively few K–12 students express interest in pursuing these subjects in college or as a career; and the performance of US students on international comparative assessments is below what many feel is adequate, given how expertise in these subjects helps fuel the nation's innovation engine. Might integrated STEM education be part of the solution to the country's math and science education woes?

There are many more questions than answers. Research on integrated STEM education is just emerging as a distinct topic. As noted, few data convincingly correlate integrated STEM education with student outcomes. Additionally, much of the research that has been conducted does not distin-

—

[2] The committee uses "problem solving" here as it is described in the cognitive science literature. For additional background, see Mayer 1992; Newell and Simon 1972; and Polya 1973.

guish between the different possible curriculum approaches and pedagogical methods for enabling integration or between the different cognitive mechanisms students may use to construct meaning from integrated learning experiences.

Taking into account these various limitations, this chapter presents the committee's findings and recommendations in four areas: research on integrated STEM education; outcomes of integrated STEM education; the nature of integrated STEM education; and the design and implementation of integrated STEM education. In some cases, the recommendations are directed to researchers, in others to those who design, implement, or assess integrated STEM education.

In the chapter's last three sections, we pose important questions for researchers in education and the learning sciences. Taken together, the questions constitute a research agenda for advancing understanding and the effective design and implementation of integrated STEM education in the United States. Addressing some of the questions will benefit from, if not require, the participation of K–12 educators who are engaged in efforts to integrate the STEM subjects.

FINDINGS AND RECOMMENDATIONS RELATED TO RESEARCH ON INTEGRATED STEM EDUCATION

In the majority of studies of curricula and programs in integrated STEM education, whether in formal or out-of-/after-school settings, the educational interventions are poorly described. Evaluation studies are of little value if it is not possible to tell what was done to improve students' understanding, skills, or attitudes. Lack of detailed descriptions of interventions and of experimental methods makes it difficult to have confidence in reported outcomes or to identify the essential ingredients of effective integrated STEM education. In addition, many of the studies used research designs or outcome measures that did not appear optimal for addressing the questions posed. Last, most studies did not have control groups, making it impossible to disentangle program effects from student selection effects.

RECOMMENDATION 1: In future studies of integrated STEM education, researchers need to document the curriculum, program, or other intervention in greater detail, with particular attention to the nature of the integration and how it was supported. When reporting on outcomes, researchers should be explicit about the nature of the integration, the types of scaffolds and instructional designs used, and the type of evidence collected to demonstrate whether the goals of the intervention were achieved. Specific learning mechanisms should be articulated and supporting evidence provided for them.

Across studies of integrated STEM education, there is often inconsistent use of language, failure to define terms, and lack of a theoretical framework for understanding integrated STEM education. One goal of this report is to provide a common vocabulary and a starting point for a theoretical framework. Generally recognized theoretical perspectives can be a powerful tool for helping build a community of researchers, program designers, and practitioners who are working toward a shared understanding. Chapter 2's descriptive framework, which suggests four high-level dimensions of integrated STEM education, provides a vocabulary that practitioners and researchers can use as a basis for mutual understanding; the implications of the research reviewed by the committee presented in Chapter 4 can be a foundation for implementation efforts as well as a basis for further research.

RECOMMENDATION 2: Researchers, program designers, and practitioners focused on integrated STEM education, and the professional organizations that represent them, need to develop a common language to describe their work. This report can serve as a starting point.

The research literature reviewed by the committee shows that studies of integrated STEM education vary greatly in design and methodology. In some cases, the study design was not suited to addressing the questions posed in the research. A recent report by education staff at the Institute for Education Sciences at the Department of Education and the National Science Foundation clarifies the categories of education research and provides basic guidance about their purposes, justifications, design features, and expected outcomes (Box 6-1). Importantly, the document notes that, although the study types are presented in a linear sequence, the reality of education research is considerably more complex and often involves multiple feedback loops between and among the categories. The two agencies intend to use the document to establish uniform expectations for proposals submitted in response to particular program announcements, solicitations, or other funding opportunities. Research teams engaged in efforts to understand integrated STEM education could benefit greatly by attending to the guid-

---

BOX 6-1
Types of Educational Research

Foundational Research and Early-Stage or Exploratory Research
contributes to *core knowledge* in education. *Core knowledge* includes basic understandings of teaching and learning, such as cognition; components and processes involved in learning and instruction; the operation of education systems; and models of systems and processes.

> *Research Type #1: Foundational Research* provides the fundamental knowledge that may contribute to improved learning and other relevant education outcomes. Studies of this type seek to test, develop, or refine theories of teaching or learning and may develop innovations in methodologies and/or technologies that will influence and inform research and development in different contexts.

> *Research Type #2: Early-Stage or Exploratory Research* examines relationships among important constructs in education and learning to establish logical connections that may form the basis for future interventions or strategies to improve education outcomes. These connections are usually correlational rather than causal.

Research Type #3: Design and Development Research develops solutions to achieve a goal related to education or learning, such as improving student engagement or mastery of a set of skills. Research projects of this type draw on existing theory and evidence to design and iteratively develop interventions or strategies, including testing individual components to provide feedback in the development process. These projects may include pilot tests of fully developed interventions to determine whether they achieve their intended outcomes under various conditions. Results from these studies could lead to additional work to better understand the foundational theory behind the results or could indicate that the intervention or strategy is sufficiently promising to warrant more advanced testing.

Impact Research contributes to evidence of impact, generating reliable estimates of the ability of a fully developed intervention or strategy to achieve its intended outcomes. The three types of *Impact Research* share many similarities of approach, including designs that eliminate or reduce bias arising from self-selection into treatment and control conditions, clearly specified outcome measures, adequate statistical power to detect

continued

BOX 6-1 Continued

effects, and data on implementation of the intervention or strategy and the counterfactual condition. However, these studies vary with regard to the conditions under which the intervention is implemented and the populations to which the findings generalize.

Research Type #4: Efficacy Research allows for testing of a strategy or intervention under "ideal" circumstances, including with a higher level of support or developer involvement than would be the case under normal circumstances. Efficacy research studies may choose to limit the investigation to a single population of interest.

Research Type #5: Effectiveness Research examines effectiveness of a strategy or intervention under circumstances that would typically prevail in the target context. The importance of "typical" circumstances means that there should not be more substantial developer support than in normal implementation, and there should not be substantial developer involvement in the evaluation of the strategy or intervention.

Research Type #6: Scale-up Research examines effectiveness in a wide range of populations, contexts, and circumstances, without substantial developer involvement in implementation or evaluation. As with effectiveness research, scale-up research should be carried out with no more developer involvement than what would be expected under typical implementation.

SOURCE: Adapted from IES/NSF (2013).

---

ance presented in this framework. Similarly, the composition of the teams, which will vary according to the category of research, can be informed by the considerations discussed in the agencies' report.

FINDINGS AND RECOMMENDATIONS RELATED TO THE OUTCOMES OF INTEGRATED STEM EDUCATION

Advocates of integrated STEM education claim that integrated approaches can produce improvements across a range of outcomes, including learning and achievement, interest, identity, and persistence in STEM fields. Yet research on these outcomes is uneven and lacks consistency in terms of definitions and variables. Studies in formal settings tend to emphasize learning outcomes, for which measures are narrowly focused on improved conceptual knowledge or achievement. In contrast, studies in after-/out-of-school settings tend to give more emphasis to outcomes related to development of interest and identity. In both settings, there is some attention to persistence in STEM, but few studies follow students over multiple years. Thus it is unclear why and how integration might offer better support for developing certain conceptual knowledge and skills. And while there is a theoretical basis for the conjecture that integrated instruction can promote stronger engagement and longer-term interest in STEM subjects, there is a lack of empirical support for this conjecture.

To determine what forms of integration are most effective, more attention needs to be directed to the types of outcome measures collected. For example, if a particular integrated STEM program focuses on science and engineering, the researchers should include separate measures of learning for each. Similarly, the differences between programs may be apparent not simply in measures of basic knowledge, such as recall of normative ideas or very contextualized problem solutions, but also in measures of deep, connected conceptual understanding and transfer. Too few studies measure retention or transfer of learning. Finally, hypothesized benefits of long-term engagement in STEM and participation in the STEM pipeline are often cited as the rationale for integrated STEM instruction. But persistent changes in attitudes, the development of STEM identities, and subsequent course taking are rarely measured in evaluations of such programs. The emerging domain of discipline-based education research is attending to many of these issues (NRC 2012a).

> **RECOMMENDATION 3**: Study outcomes should be identified from the outset based on clearly articulated hypotheses about the mechanisms by which integrated STEM education supports learning, thinking, interest, identity, and persistence. Measures should be selected or developed based on these outcomes.

Learning, Reasoning, and Achievement

In studies on integrated STEM education, learning outcomes are often measured using scores on standardized tests, though some studies include tests of knowledge specifically tied to the intervention. For outcomes that are more typically measured, such as gains in content knowledge, it is important to be sure that the measure fits the expected outcomes; achievement tests are often used, but a more refined measure directly linked to the particular experience may be more appropriate. Outcomes tested might relate to students' ability to make connections between disciplines or to use concepts or skills learned in the context of one discipline in the context of a different discipline. Such outcomes are likely very difficult to measure but more reflective of the deeper learning many experts believe is vital for college and career readiness (NRC 2012b).

Interest, Identity, and Persistence

Understanding the impact of integrated STEM education on learners' attitudes about the disciplines is important and will help determine whether integrated STEM environments can be more interesting and motivating for students than settings in which there is no integration. In its review of the literature, the committee found hints that integrated STEM education may positively influence STEM interest and identity, and that this effect may be particularly strong for populations that have historically struggled in STEM classes and are underrepresented in STEM programs in higher education and STEM professions.

As noted in Chapter 3, identity generally refers to who one is or wants to be, as well as to how one is recognized by others—as a particular kind of person with particular interests, expertise, and ways of being in particular social contexts. Preliminary evidence indicates that problem- and inquiry-based work better position youth in expert roles, especially when students can define the content and direction of the research. Integrated experiences also appear to offer a wider range of knowledge, experience, and ways of knowing that might be valued by schools and employers and that are integral to identity development. However, more research is needed to determine if this is the case across different populations and contexts.

All but two of the studies on identity that the committee reviewed were qualitative in nature, and most were ethnographic. Ethnography is a clear choice for documenting local settings in rich detail with in-depth focus on individuals, resources, tools, actions, and interactions. Most of the studies took place over several months (some were shorter term, and several longer). Few of the studies seriously considered race or class as central analytic lenses, even if the students involved were of different races and ethnicities. The few longer-term studies and small sample sizes limit the ability to understand patterns of identity development and the mechanisms that lead to productive patterns.

RECOMMENDATION 4: Research on integrated STEM education that is focused on interest and identity should include more longitudinal studies, use multiple methods, including design experiments, and address diversity and equity.

An underlying assumption of the focus on interest and identity is that students with greater interest in STEM and who identify with STEM will be more likely to seek and persist in STEM-related experiences, not only through traditional or interdisciplinary career paths but also by using their STEM knowledge and skills in other professions and pursuits. This has typically been measured by tracking course taking after an integrated STEM experience or through self-reported aspirations. In the case of integrated STEM education programs in after- and out-of-school settings, most of the studies that measured persistence did not include a sufficient control or comparison group of students who did not participate in the program to enable inferences about impact. Because students in after-/out-of-school programs can choose whether to participate, it is important to design studies that support inferences about the role of the integrated STEM programs in persistence in STEM.

Box 6-2 provides examples of research questions related to the outcomes of integrated STEM education.

FINDINGS RELATED TO THE NATURE OF INTEGRATED STEM EDUCATION

Our analysis of the research and examination of specific programs led to important findings about three aspects of integrated STEM education: the interplay between integrated and disciplinary learning; the cognitive pluses and minuses associated with connection making; and the role that context seems to play in supporting integrated STEM learning.

One reasonable expectation of integrated STEM education is that it encourages the learner to make new and useful connections between or among STEM disciplines. These connections may be exhibited as improvements in student performance, learning and transfer, and interest and moti-

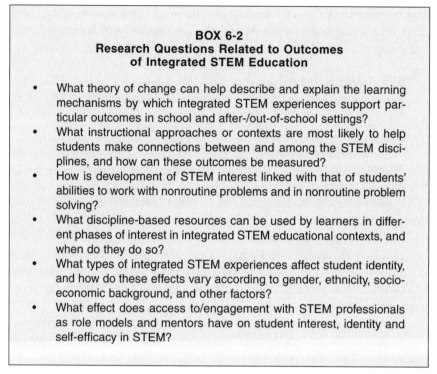

BOX 6-2
Research Questions Related to Outcomes
of Integrated STEM Education

- What theory of change can help describe and explain the learning mechanisms by which integrated STEM experiences support particular outcomes in school and after-/out-of-school settings?
- What instructional approaches or contexts are most likely to help students make connections between and among the STEM disciplines, and how can these outcomes be measured?
- How is development of STEM interest linked with that of students' abilities to work with nonroutine problems and in nonroutine problem solving?
- What discipline-based resources can be used by learners in different phases of interest in integrated STEM educational contexts, and when do they do so?
- What types of integrated STEM experiences affect student identity, and how do these effects vary according to gender, ethnicity, socioeconomic background, and other factors?
- What effect does access to/engagement with STEM professionals as role models and mentors have on student interest, identity and self-efficacy in STEM?

vation. Some research suggests that integration can support learning because basic qualities of cognition favor connecting concepts and representations, so they are associated with other knowledge and grounded in familiar experiences and prior knowledge. Yet the literature is also full of examples suggesting that integration requires considerable cognitive resources. Thus, in some cases activities that integrate multiple disciplines may actually impede comprehension and learning because of the large mental processing demands associated with split attention—dividing one's attention between multiple sources of information presented in noncomplementary forms, in different settings, or at different times.

Our review of the research suggests that, to benefit from integrated STEM education experiences, students need to be competent with discipline-specific representations and able to translate between them, exhibiting what some scholars refer to as "representational fluency." Participation in shared practices, such as modeling in engineering, science, and mathematics, may support such fluency. But because the practice of modeling differs in these disciplines, it is possible that shared practices might actually muddle important distinctions. The level of disciplinary competency may be fairly low in younger students and still allow meaningful integrated STEM experiences; higher levels of content knowledge become increasingly important as students move into high school and tackle more challenging problems. To help students both build and use disciplinary knowledge and skill in integrated settings, it may be necessary to strategically incorporate discipline-specific learning opportunities into integrated experiences (see, for example, Burghardt and Hacker 2008; Lehrer and Schauble 2004).

The use of problem solving as a context and pedagogical approach for integrating concepts and practices from multiple disciplines is a feature of many integrated STEM education programs. One implication of this finding is that practices such as engineering design and science inquiry, and instructional approaches like problem- and project-based learning, may offer special opportunities to support STEM integration when sufficient and intentional instructional support is provided. Some problem situations aim for authenticity, but there are also contrived problems that may support student learning, and some authentic problems will be too complex to carry out in the classroom. Working on complex, authentic problems, which almost always calls upon multiple disciplines, has the potential to support both short-term learning and longer-term application or transfer to new contexts. However, such outcomes are not a given and depend on a number of factors related to the design and implementation of the learning experience, as well as the teacher's ability to successfully support student problem-solving efforts.

Box 6-3 provides examples of research questions related to the nature of integrated STEM education.

FINDINGS AND RECOMMENDATIONS RELATED TO THE DESIGN AND IMPLEMENTATION OF INTEGRATED STEM EDUCATION

Those who design and implement integrated STEM education experiences will need to attend to a number of interrelated factors, if they hope to influence student learning, interest, motivation, and persistence in STEM subjects. A starting point can be the committee's effort in Chapter 4 to spell out the implications of the research for creating or modifying existing STEM education programs to include elements of disciplinary integration. The

---

BOX 6-3
Research Questions Related to the Nature
of Integrated STEM Education

- What disciplinary knowledge that is important to success in later STEM-related study or work can be learned in an integrated setting, and what disciplinary knowledge is best learned in more traditional ways?
- What features of integrated STEM learning experiences support and what features impede the learner's ability to make connections between or among disciplinary ideas and/or practices?
- When problem solving is used as a context for integrated STEM education, to what extent and in what situations are student learning and other valued outcomes attributable to the integration versus situating the material in a real-world context?
- How, if at all, and in what circumstances does the use of engineering design in integrated STEM education boost learning, motivation, or interest in science and mathematics beyond that resulting from high-quality instruction in those subjects not involving engineering design?
- Is there a repertoire of high-level, cross-domain abilities—such as complex reasoning and problem solving—rooted in the STEM disciplines that can be strengthened through integrated learning approaches?
- To what degree might these abilities be transferable or generalizable to academic subjects or workplace domains outside STEM?
- What synergistic STEM concepts and practices are learned better through integrated STEM education approaches than via disciplinary-focused approaches, and what student and teacher supports are needed to accomplish this learning?

---

potential benefits and challenges of making connections across the STEM subjects suggest the importance of a measured, strategic approach to implementing integrated STEM education that accounts for the inherent trade-offs in cognition and learning.

Beyond this, being clear up front about what an educational intervention is expected to achieve—goal setting—is critical. As noted, we found that the goals of integrated STEM education in formal settings are often focused on achievement and preparation for future academic study. In after-/out-of-school settings, the goals of integrated STEM education tend to focus on promoting awareness and interest in the STEM disciplines more than on academic achievement and preparation for future study or careers. The majority of integrated STEM education programs reviewed by the committee did not explicitly tie goals to hypotheses about the design of the intervention. This makes it very difficult to determine whether integration is helping to achieve the particular goal.

> **RECOMMENDATION 5**: Designers of integrated STEM education initiatives need to be explicit about the goals they aim to achieve and design the integrated STEM experience purposefully to achieve these goals. They also need to better articulate their hypotheses about why and how a particular integrated STEM experience will lead to particular outcomes and how those outcomes should be measured.

As noted, there are few studies that specify and test the mechanisms by which integrated STEM experiences support learning within and across the disciplines. In this report we have begun to describe potential mechanisms based on existing research on learning in integrated settings and more broadly. One example of such a mechanism is to look for core concepts and practices that recur in the STEM subjects. Such recurring concepts and practices can be elaborated, extended, or otherwise transformed by exploring the different senses of the "same" idea or practice across multiple STEM disciplines. Designing educational initiatives to take advantage of these recurring ideas and practices is challenging. Many of the practices, such as developing and using models, and crosscutting concepts, such as patterns and systems, identified in *A Framework for K–12 Science Education* (NRC 2012c) may be good candidates.

It is clear from the research that STEM connections that may appear obvious to teachers, curriculum developers, and disciplinary experts often are not obvious to novice learners. At times, teachers themselves may not apprehend the connections. For either reason, integration of STEM concepts and transfer of learning to new contexts may not be spontaneously made by students and cannot be assumed to take place simply because certain concepts and practices are introduced at the same time or place. Put another way, deep, lasting, and transferable learning through integrative experiences will rarely be automatic for most students and some teachers.

> **RECOMMENDATION 6**: Designers of integrated STEM education initiatives need to build in opportunities that make STEM connections

explicit to students and educators (e.g., through appropriate scaffolding and sufficient opportunities to engage in activities that address connected ideas).

As previously noted, neither the committee nor this report is suggesting that integrated STEM education take the place of high-quality education focused on the individual STEM subjects. Indeed, if anything, integrated STEM education reinforces the need for students to hone their disciplinary expertise.

RECOMMENDATION 7: Designers of integrated STEM experiences need to attend to the learning goals and learning progressions in the individual STEM subjects so as not to inadvertently undermine student learning in those subjects.

It seems clear that implementing integrated STEM experiences in school and after-/out-of-school settings will often require educator expertise beyond that required to teach any of the STEM disciplines alone. This finding has implications for the education and ongoing support of those charged with delivering integrated STEM instruction.

RECOMMENDATION 8: Programs that prepare people to deliver integrated STEM instruction need to provide experiences that help these educators identify and make explicit to their students connections among the disciplines. These educators will also need opportunities and training to work collaboratively with their colleagues, and in some cases administrators or curriculum coordinators will need to play a role in creating these opportunities. Finally, some forms of professional development may need to be designed as partnerships among educators, STEM professionals, and researchers.

A growing number of K–12 schools self-identify as "STEM" schools, and some proportion of these schools are or claim to be delivering integrated STEM education. For schools attempting integrated STEM education as well as for those, such as private funders, with a desire to support such efforts, this report can provide a useful guide for assessing the nature and degree of integration present. The committee's effort to map one school's efforts against the descriptive framework for integrated STEM education (see Table 2-1, p. 48) is an example of how this might be done.

Assessment

The design and implementation of any educational intervention will benefit by having methods or tools for assessing outcomes. Without a way of determining how student understanding of STEM concepts and facility with STEM practices are changing, it will be impossible to modify the design or implementation in ways that improve chances for success. In the case of integrated STEM education, we have found no evidence that researchers, curriculum developers, or practitioners are measuring outcomes from integrated STEM experiences in reliable, valid ways. The National Assessment of Educational Progress will field an assessment of technology and engineering literacy in a sample of US 8th graders in 2014 (NAEP 2013). While the test will not probe connections among the STEM subjects per se, it will measure performance on problem-solving activities. Lessons learned from this assessment may be useful to future efforts to develop assessments for integrated STEM education. In addition, as the NGSS begin to be adopted and implemented by the states, pressure for new assessments, including those that measure facets of STEM integration, may increase. The National Research Council has developed a framework for assessment of K–12 science proficiency based on NGSS that addresses issues of integration.[3]

> **RECOMMENDATION 9**: Organizations with expertise in assessment research and development should create assessments appropriate to measuring the various learning and affective outcomes of integrated STEM education. This work should involve not only the modification of existing tools and techniques but also exploration of novel approaches. Federal agencies with a major role in supporting STEM education in the United States, such as the Department of Education and the National Science Foundation, should consider supporting these efforts.

In order for any significant and lasting change to take hold within the K–12 education system, decades of research and experience suggest the importance of aligning key aspects of the improvement process. Thus, for example, both the design of an educational intervention and its implementation should reflect the goals and objectives established by the developers (e.g., Krajcik et al. 2008). Furthermore, what is learned during implementation and data gathered on the outcomes of the intervention should inform an iterative process of con-

---

[3] Information on the project is available at www8.nationalacademies.org/cp/projectview. aspx?key=49464.

tinuous improvement (see, for example, NRC 2003). The design, implementation, and even the original goals may need to be modified to reflect experience and optimize the desired outcomes. These ideas can be represented as a series of feedback loops (Figure 6-1).

The challenge of creating alignment and assuring productive feedback among the major elements of education change is not trivial. As the committee notes in its review of the research on STEM education in Chapter 3 and repeats in this chapter, many well-meaning efforts to develop integrated STEM education programs are either unclear about goals or do not collect outcomes data that allow one to determine if the stated goals have been met. In addition, in many cases, it is not possible to determine if the program as

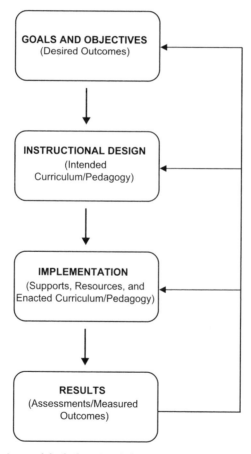

FIGURE 6-1 Iterative model of educational change.

designed, what is sometimes called the intended curriculum, is the same as what is implemented, the enacted curriculum.

RECOMMENDATION 10: To allow for continuous and meaningful improvement, designers of integrated STEM education initiatives, those charged with implementing such efforts, and organizations that fund the interventions should explicitly ground their efforts in an iterative model of educational improvement.

Box 6-4 provides examples of research questions related to the design and implementation of integrated STEM education.

BOX 6-4
Research Questions Related to the Design and
Implementation of Integrated STEM Education

- What discipline-based resources do learners make use of in integrated contexts and, when they do so, what supports are needed and how can integration be facilitated?
- What age-related developmental strengths and needs exist in different types of integrated learning situations?
- How are problem-solving experiences best constructed to support student learning and other desired outcomes in integrated STEM education?
- How should integrated STEM experiences be designed to account for educators' and students' varying levels of experience with integrated learning and STEM content?
- What pedagogical content knowledge do educators require to successfully support student learning in integrated STEM education experiences, and how might this knowledge vary according to student age or level of interest in STEM?
- What pedagogical practices best support student learning in integrated STEM education?
- What are the benefits and trade-offs of delivering integrated STEM education experiences with collaborative teams of educators who have expertise in different STEM disciplines?
- Given the variability in teachers' own knowledge of STEM content and pedagogy, what kinds of instructional supports might be most effective and most useful for them?
- What features of a school's management, organization, philosophy, and physical facilities are most important to supporting teachers and students in integrated approaches to STEM education?

Two recent developments in US K–12 STEM education provide special opportunities for researchers to investigate some of these questions. One, as noted above, is publication of the NGSS, which is spurring new curriculum, assessments, and educator supports, some of which will focus on how science and engineering concepts and practices are connected. The second is the implementation of restructured advanced placement (AP) science courses by the College Board, developed in response to recommendations from the National Research Council (2002).The new AP biology course was introduced in the 2012-13 school year (College Board 2011a) and the new chemistry course in 2013-14 (College Board 2011b). The revised physics course will begin in the 2014-15 school year, and the environmental science course sometime after 2015. Although each of these courses has a disciplinary emphasis, they also aim to build student competencies to connect with other subjects, particularly mathematics.

FINAL THOUGHTS

In addressing its charge, the committee has carefully reviewed the available research on integrated STEM education and related research and examined a selected set of curricula, schools, professional development efforts, and other relevant initiatives. As this final chapter suggests, there is much more that can and should be learned about the outcomes, nature, and design and implementation of integrated STEM education. This should not discourage those designing, implementing, or studying integrated STEM education programs. On the contrary, our findings, recommendations, and research agenda strongly suggest the *potential* of some forms of integrated STEM education to make a positive difference in student learning, interest, and other valued outcomes.

In order to achieve this potential, the energy, creativity, and resources of researchers, practitioners, and concerned funders must now be directed at generating more thoughtful, high-quality, and evidence-based work. Given the inherent complexities, it will not be a surprise to find that designing, implementing, and documenting effective integrated STEM education is both time consuming and expensive. Despite these very real challenges, the possibility of adding new tools to the STEM education toolbox is tantalizing.

REFERENCES

AACU (Association of American Colleges and Universities). 2013. It takes more than a major: Employer priorities for college learning and student success. Available at www.aacu.org/leap/documents/2013_EmployerSurvey.pdf (retrieved January 21, 2014).

Achieve, Inc. 2013. Next Generation Science Standards. Available at www.nextgenscience.org/next-generation-science-standards (retrieved May 31, 2013).

Burghardt, D., and M. Hacker. 2008. Work in progress: Math infusion in a middle school engineering/technology class. 38th ASEE/IEEE Frontiers in Education Conference, October 22–25, 2008, Saratoga Springs, NY. Available at http://ieeexplore.ieee.org/stamp/stamp.jsp?arnumber=4720457 (retrieved May 2, 2013).

Carnevale, A.P., N. Smith, and M. Melton. 2011. STEM. Georgetown University Center on Education and the Workforce. Available at www9.georgetown.edu/grad/gppi/hpi/cew/pdfs/stem-complete.pdf. (retrieved May 26, 2013).

College Board. 2011a. AP Biology Curriculum Framework 2012-2013. New York. The College Board. Available at http://media.collegeboard.com/digitalServices/pdf/ap/10b_2727_AP_Biology_CF_WEB_110128.pdf (retrieved November 11, 2013).

College Board. 2011b. AP Chemistry Curriculum Framework 2013-2014. New York: The College Board. Available at http://media.collegeboard.com/digitalServices/pdf/ap/11_3461_AP_CF_Chemistry_WEB_110930.pdf (retrieved November 11, 2013).

IES (Institute for Educational Sciences)/NSF (National Science Foundation). 2013. Common guidelines for education research and development—A report from the Institute of Education Sciences, U.S. Department of Education and the National Science Foundation. August 2013. Available at http://ies.ed.gov/pdf/CommonGuidelines.pdf (retrieved October 30, 2013).

Krajcik, J., K.L. McNeill, and B. Reiser. 2008. Learning-goals-driven design model: Developing curriculum materials that align with national standards and incorporate project-based pedagogy. Science Education 92(1):1–32.

Lehrer, R., and L. Schauble. 2004. Modeling natural variation through distribution. American Educational Research Journal 41(3):635–679.

Mayer, R.E. 1992. Thinking, problem solving, cognition. New York: W.H. Freeman.

NAEP (National Assessment of Educational Progress. 2013. NAEP Technology and Engineering Literacy Assessment (TEL). Available at http://nces.ed.gov/nationsreportcard/tel/ (retrieved June 11, 2013).

Newell, A., and H.A. Simon. 1972. Human problem solving. Englewood Cliffs, NJ: Prentice-Hall.

Polya, G. 1973. How to solve it: A new aspect of mathematical method. Princeton, NJ: Princeton University Press.

NRC (National Research Council). 2002. Learning and understanding: Improving advanced study of mathematics and science in U.S. high schools. J.P. Gollub, M.W. Bertenthal, J.B. Labov, and P.C. Curtis, Eds. Available at www.nap.edu/catalog.php?record_id=10129 (retrieved November 11, 2013).

NRC. 2003. Strategic Education Research Partnership. Available at www.nap.edu/catalog.php?record_id=10670 (retrieved January 16, 2013).

NRC. 2012a. Discipline-based education research: Understanding and improving learning in undergraduate science and engineering. Committee on the Status, Contributions, and Future Directions of Discipline-Based Education Research, Board on Science Education, Division of Behavioral and Social Sciences and Education. S.R. Singer, N.R. Nielsen, and H.A. Schweingruber, Eds. Available at www.nap.edu/catalog.php?record_id=13362 (retrieved May 30, 2013).

NRC. 2012b. Education for life and work: Developing transferable knowledge and skills in the 21st century. Committee on Defining Deeper Learning and 21st Century Skills. Available at www.nap.edu/catalog.php?record_id=13398 (retrieved May 31, 2013).

NRC. 2012c. A Framework for K–12 Science Education. Available at www.nap.edu/catalog.php?record_id=13165 (retrieved January 14, 2014).

Appendix

Biographies of Committee Members

Dr. Margaret A. Honey
New York Hall of Science

Margaret Honey, *chair*, is president and CEO of the New York Hall of Science, where she is interested in the role of design-based learning in promoting student interest and achievement in STEM subjects. Before joining the museum in November 2008, she was vice president of the Education Development Center (EDC) and director of its Center for Children and Technology. During her 15 years at EDC, she was the architect and overseer of numerous large-scale projects funded by the National Science Foundation, Institute for Education Sciences, Carnegie Corporation, Library of Congress, US Department of Education, and US Department of Energy. She also codirected the Regional Educational Laboratory–Northeast and Islands, helping educators, policymakers, and communities improve schools by leveraging research findings about learning and K–12 education.

Dr. Honey is widely recognized for using digital technologies to support children's learning in the STEM disciplines. Her work has shaped thinking about learning and technology with special attention to traditionally underserved audiences. She has led some of the country's most innovative and successful education research, focusing on efforts to identify teaching practices and assessments for 21st century skills; new approaches to teaching computational science in high schools; collaborations with PBS,

CPB, and national public television stations; investigations of data-driven decision-making tools and practices; and, with colleagues at Bank Street College of Education, the creation of one of the first Internet-based professional development programs in the country.

Dr. Honey has shared what she's learned before Congress, state legislatures, and federal panels and in numerous articles, chapters, and books. She is a member of the National Research Council's Board on Science Education, chaired an NRC[1] workshop that resulted in the report *IT Fluency and High School Graduation Outcomes*, and coedited *Learning Science: Computer Games, Simulations, and Education*. Her 2013 book *Design, Make, Play: Growing the Next Generation of STEM Innovators* (coedited with David Kanter) explores the potential of these strategies for supporting student engagement and deeper learning. She is a graduate of Hampshire College and earned her doctorate in developmental psychology from Columbia University.

Dr. Linda M. Abriola
Tufts University

Linda Abriola is dean of the School of Engineering at Tufts University as well as professor of civil and environmental engineering and adjunct professor in chemical and biological engineering. She is a member of both the National Academy of Engineering (NAE) and the American Academy of Arts and Sciences (AAAS) and a fellow of the American Geophysical Union. Before her appointment at Tufts, she was the Horace Williams King Collegiate Professor of Environmental Engineering at the University of Michigan. Her research focuses on the integration of mathematical modeling and laboratory experiments for the investigation and prediction of the transport and fate of reactive contaminants in the subsurface. An author of more than 130 refereed publications, she is particularly known for her work on the characterization and remediation of aquifers contaminated by chlorinated solvents. Dr. Abriola's numerous professional activities have included service on the US Environmental Protection Agency Science Advisory Board, the NRC Water Science and Technology Board, and the US Department of Energy's Natural and Accelerated Bioremediation Research (NABIR) Advisory Committee. She served on the NRC's Committee on Ground Water Cleanup Alternatives, which investigated the

---

[1] Here and throughout, NRC designates the National Research Council unless otherwise indicated.

efficacy of pump-and-treat technologies; Committee on Gender Differences in Careers of Science, Engineering, and Mathematics Faculty; and the NAE Offshoring Engineering Workshop Committee. She is the recipient of numerous honors, including the Association for Women Geoscientists' Outstanding Educator Award (1996), the National Ground Water Association's Distinguished Darcy Lectureship (1996), and the Strategic Environmental Research and Development Program (SERDP) Project of the Year Award in Environmental Restoration (2006 and 2012) and was named Drexel University's Engineering Leader of the Year in 2013. Dean Abriola received her PhD and master's degree from Princeton University and a bachelor's degree from Drexel University, all in civil engineering.

Dr. Sybilla Beckmann
University of Georgia

Sybilla Beckmann, Josiah Meigs Distinguished Teaching Professor of Mathematics at the University of Georgia, has done research in arithmetic geometry but is currently interested in the mathematical education of teachers and mathematics content for students at all levels, especially pre-K through the middle grades. She is interested in helping college faculty learn to teach mathematics content courses for elementary and middle school teachers and works with graduate students and postdoctoral fellows toward that end. She developed mathematics content courses for prospective elementary school teachers at the University of Georgia, wrote a book for such courses, *Mathematics for Elementary Teachers*, now in its fourth edition, and is studying future middle school teachers' thinking and learning about proportional relationships. She has worked on the development of several states' mathematics standards. In addition, Beckmann was a member of the writing team of the National Council of Teachers of Mathematics (NCTM)'s *Curriculum Focal Points for Prekindergarten through Grade 8 Mathematics*, the mathematics writing team for the Common Core State Standards Initiative, and the NRC committee that produced the report *Mathematics Learning in Early Childhood: Paths Toward Excellence and Equity*. She taught at Yale University as J.W. Gibbs Instructor of Mathematics and also taught an average 6th grade mathematics class at a local public school in order to better understand school mathematics teaching. She earned her PhD in mathematics from the University of Pennsylvania.

Dr. Susan Hackwood
California Council on Science and Technology

Susan Hackwood is executive director of the California Council on Science and Technology (CCST) and professor of electrical engineering at the University of California, Riverside, where in 1990 she was the founding dean of Bourns College of Engineering. In 2003–2005 she was a visiting scholar at UCLA's Anderson School of Management and in 2005 a visiting scholar at the California Institute of Technology. In 1984 she joined the University of California, Santa Barbara, as professor of electrical and computer engineering and was founder and director of the National Science Foundation Engineering Research Center for Robotic Systems in Microelectronics (CRSM). Before joining academia, she was department head of device robotics technology research at AT&T Bell Labs, where, among other things, she invented and named the electrowetting effect, now used in many micro devices and an increasing number of applications. Her current research interests are science and technology policy, innovation mechanisms, and distributed asynchronous and cellular robotic systems. She has worked extensively with industry, academia, and government partnerships to identify policy issues of societal importance. She is also active in regional, state, national, and international economic, science, and technology development (e.g., in Mexico, Taiwan, Vietnam, and Costa Rica). She is a fellow of the IEEE and the AAAS. For the AAAS, she has served as engineering delegate and chaired the Committee on Science, Engineering, and Public Policy and the section on Societal Impacts of Science and Engineering. Since 2006 she has been a member of the IEEE Spectrum Editorial Board. She also serves on the boards of directors and consults on new product development for several technology companies. She cofounded and coedited the *Journal of Robotic Systems* from 1984 to 2005. She received her PhD in solid-state ionics in 1979 from DeMontfort University, UK, and holds honorary degrees from Worcester Polytechnic Institute (PhD) and DeMontfort University (DSc).

Dr. Alfred L. Hall II
University of Memphis

Alfred Hall is an assistant professor of science education at the University of Memphis, where he is also director of the West Tennessee STEM Collaboratory Hub. He was previously chief of staff for the Memphis city schools system and served the district in other capacities, such as chief academic officer, associate superintendent of curriculum and instruction, and director of mathematics and science, for a school system of 106,000 students and more than 7,000 teachers. He began his educational career as a high school teacher of biology and physics and an instructor of biology and program director for an undergraduate STEM program for underrepresented students at Delta State University in Cleveland, Mississippi. He has also worked as a science education specialist for the Eisenhower Mathematics and Science Consortium at Appalachia Educational Laboratory, which supported state education agencies and school districts in Kentucky, Tennessee, Virginia, and West Virginia. In 1999 he was selected to serve as project director of the Delta Rural Systemic Initiative, a reform program funded by the National Science Foundation to support poor, rural school districts in the delta areas of Arkansas, Louisiana, and Mississippi. In 2001, he began directing the Memphis Urban Systemic Program and provided leadership for mathematics and science education, teacher professional development, and student support programs. He has served on the National Science Advisory Board for Macmillan/McGraw-Hill Publishing Company and the National Task Force for Recruiting, Retaining, and Supporting Teachers of Mathematics for the National Council of Teachers of Mathematics. He received his PhD in science education from George Mason University.

Dr. Jennifer Hicks
I-STEM Resource Network

Jennifer Hicks is K–12 science program manager for Purdue University's I-STEM Resource Network, managing professional development and curriculum implementation for the Indiana Science Initiative, a K–8 systemic science initiative that has engaged 2,000 teachers and 134 schools in research-developed science curriculum and professional development. Prior to this position she was science curriculum specialist in the Office of Curriculum and Instruction for the Indiana Department of Education, where she managed the development of science standards, supported curriculum resources for science, and promoted innovation in science teaching throughout the state. A former high school teacher in California, she received a Life Sciences Single Subject Credential from San Francisco State University. She also holds a Professional Educator's License in the State of Indiana in chemistry and life sciences. She has taught biology, chemistry, marine biology, and Earth sciences at the high school level and science at the postsecondary and graduate levels at Webster University in St. Louis and at Indiana University in Bloomington. With a BS in biology and a PhD in visual sciences from Indiana University, she was an NIH postdoctoral fellow in the Biology Department at Washington University in St. Louis, where she performed research on proteins in fruit flies.

Mr. Stephen J. Krak
Battelle

Steve Krak is an open innovation manager for Battelle's energy and environment business, responsible for intellectual property management and business development. He began his 25-year career at Battelle as an electrical engineering intern and has handled assignments in photonics and microfabrication R&D, project management, line management, business development (domestic and international), and intellectual property management. He is a long-time volunteer in the classroom and served four years as founding program manager of the Ohio STEM Learning Network, a public-private collaboration to change the relationship between economic development, education, and personal prosperity in Ohio. He also managed the proposal process for Ohio's winning Race to the Top submission and was relationship manager to New York at the beginning of Battelle's multi-state STEM network program.

Mr. Bill Kurtz
DSST Public Schools

Bill Kurtz is founding head of school and CEO of the Denver School of Science and Technology (DSST), a charter school management organization that is opening ten secondary schools on five campuses in Denver. The flagship school of DSST Public Schools has become an exemplar for high school reform and a leader in STEM education nationwide. The combination of the school's significant year-to-year student learning growth, very diverse student population, innovative school culture, and 100 percent college acceptance rate for its graduates has made DSST a change agent for local public schools and a destination for school reformers from all over the country. Bill was recognized as the 2010 Entrepreneur of the Year by the New Schools Venture Fund at its national summit in Washington, DC, and in 2008 was named one of 25 champions of public education in Denver over the last 25 years by the Public Education Business Coalition. He serves on the advisory council of the University of Southern California's Rossier School of Education Master of Arts in Teaching (MAT) program. Before joining DSST, he was principal of Link Community School, an independent middle school in Newark, New Jersey. He graduated magna cum laude from Princeton University with a BA and earned an MA from Columbia University's Teachers College in educational administration and leadership.

Dr. Richard Lehrer
Peabody College of Vanderbilt University

Richard Lehrer is the Frank W. Mayborn Professor of Education at Vanderbilt University's Peabody College. He worked previously at the University of Wisconsin–Madison as associate director of the National Center for Improving Student Learning and Achievement in Mathematics and Science. He collaborates with teachers to craft, implement, and assess modeling approaches to mathematics and science education in the elementary and middle school grades. He has also formulated innovative geometry instruction for primary and elementary school students that is guided by longitudinal study of student thinking about space. He is a former high school science teacher and has pioneered classroom research that investigates cognitive technologies as tools for thought in mathematics and science. He has served on the NRC Committees on the Foundations of Assessment and on Systems of Statewide Science Assessment, and the NAE/NRC Committee on Engineering in K–12 Education. He has a PhD in educational psychology and statistics from the University of New York, Albany.

Ms. Beth McGrath
Stevens Institute of Technology

Beth McGrath is chief of staff in the president's office at Stevens Institute of Technology in Hoboken, NJ. She was previously executive director of the institute's Center for Innovation in Engineering and Science Education (CIESE) and senior research associate in its Schools of Engineering & Science and Systems & Enterprises. Since 2005, under her leadership, CIESE has been honored with the Presidential Award for Excellence in Mathematics, Science, and Engineering Mentoring and has garnered more than $26 million in STEM education and research projects (sponsored by the National Science Foundation, US Department of Defense, NJ Department of Education, and US Department of Education), mainly in K–12 engineering and science education, 21st century skills, and STEM scale-up and capacity building in K–12 and higher education. She played a key role in several national Internet-in-K–12 science education curriculum development and teacher training initiatives for more than 35,000 teachers in 23 states and 8 countries. Her research interests include organizational development and capacity building in K–12 education, diffusion of technology innovations in K–12, and the role of engineering in 21st century skill development. She serves on the Technology and Engineering Literacy (TEL) Assessment Standing Committee of the National Assessment of Educational Progress (NAEP) as well as several advisory boards of science and engineering education development projects. She holds a BS degree in mass communications from Virginia Commonwealth University and an MEd from the University of Maryland.

Dr. Barbara M. Means
SRI International

Barbara Means, codirector of the Center for Technology in Learning at SRI International, is a leader in defining issues and approaches for evaluating the implementation and efficacy of technology-supported educational innovations. Her research focuses on ways technology can support students' learning of advanced skills and the revitalization of classrooms and schools, and on STEM-focused secondary schools that target underserved populations and do not use selective admissions processes. In addition, she is directing SRI's work supporting the National Science Foundation's effort to implement a K–12 STEM education indicator system, as recommended by the 2013 NRC report *Monitoring Progress Toward Successful K–12 STEM Education*. Her published works include the edited volumes *Evaluating Educational Technology, Technology and Education Reform*, and *Teaching Advanced Skills to At-Risk Students* and the jointly authored volumes *Using Technology Evaluation to Advance Student Learning, The Connected School*, and *Comparative Studies of How People Think*. A fellow of the American Educational Research Association, Dr. Means serves on the boards of the Oracle Education Foundation and CFY, a nonprofit organization promoting effective uses of technology in schools that serve low-income students. She has served on the NRC Committee on Highly Successful Schools or Programs for K–12 STEM Education, Board on Testing and Assessment, and the committee that produced *How People Learn*. She earned her bachelor's degree in psychology from Stanford University and her PhD in educational psychology at the University of California, Berkeley.

Ms. Donna Migdol
Oceanside School District, New York

Donna Migdol is a 5th- and 6th-grade "project extra" elementary teacher in Oceanside, New York, where her students are passionately involved in STEM learning. She previously taught grades 3–6 and was the mathematics lead teacher and supervisor for K–6 mathematics and science. She has presented her classroom engineering design and math lessons to the Peer Review Panel in Albany and to the National Science Foundation. WNET and Teacher Net filmed her third grade classroom, highlighting engineering design coupled with inquiry-based math and science instruction, and in 2012 her fifth graders were filmed by the Teaching Channel and WNET in "Roller Coaster Physics" (www.teachingchannel.org/videos/teaching-stem-strategies). Ms. Migdol codeveloped and facilitated the Math, Science, and Technology Summer Institute at Hofstra University, where she is an adjunct professor teaching graduate STEM courses, and she partnered with Hofstra's Center for Technological Literacy as a curriculum writer and professional developer for two grant-funded projects supporting STEM literacy in grades 6–8. As keynote presenter for Hofstra's HNET Conference, she spoke about "What a classroom could be. . . ." She has also served as an elementary mathematics and STEM consultant for school districts across Long Island. She has published several articles and her work has been cited in Alfie Kohn's book, *The Schools Our Children Deserve*, as well as *Exemplary Science in Grades 5–8: Standards-Based Success Stories*, edited by Robert E. Yager.

Dr. Mitchell J. Nathan
University of Wisconsin–Madison

Mitchell Nathan is a professor of learning sciences in the Department of Educational Psychology and director of the Center on Education and Work, both at the University of Wisconsin–Madison, as well as faculty member for the Latin American School for Education, Cognitive, and Neural Sciences. He also holds affiliate appointments in the UW-Madison Department of Curriculum and Instruction, Department of Psychology, and Wisconsin Center for Education Research. In research and development in artificial intelligence, computer vision, and robotic mobility, he has worked on the design and development of autonomous robotic arms and vehicles; the development of expert systems and knowledge engineering interview techniques; and the representation of perceptual and real-world knowledge to support inference making in dynamic environments. He has also worked on computer-based mathematics tutoring that relies heavily on students' comprehension processes for self-evaluation and self-directed learning (so-called unintelligent tutoring systems). Prof. Nathan directed the project Supporting the Transition from Arithmetic to Algebraic Reasoning (STAAR; funded by the Interagency Education Research Initiative, IERI), which studied the transition from arithmetic to algebraic reasoning. He is co-PI for both the AWAKEN Project ("Aligning educational experiences with WAys of Knowing ENgineering"), which documents how people learn and use engineering, and the National Center for Cognition and Mathematics Instruction. He is a member of the steering committee for the Delta Program, which promotes the development of a national faculty in the natural and social sciences, engineering, and mathematics that is committed to implementing and advancing effective teaching practices for diverse student audiences. He received his PhD in experimental (cognitive) psychology and holds a BS in electrical and computer engineering, mathematics, and history.

Dr. Mark Sanders
Virginia Polytechnic Institute and State University

Mark Sanders, Virginia Tech Professor Emeritus of Integrative STEM Education/Technology Education, has been working for more than two decades in integrative STEM education. As co-PI of the Technology, Science, Mathematics (TSM) Integration Project (NSF, 1991–1996) he coauthored *Technology, Science, Mathematics Connection Activities* (1996, McGraw-Hill) and *Engineering & Design Applications* (2008, McGraw-Hill). In 2003, he conceptualized Virginia Tech's unique integrative STEM education graduate program, which he cofounded in 2005 and for which he continues to advise PhD candidates. From 1980 to 2005 he pioneered, disseminated, and taught emerging communication technologies, including e-publishing (1981), digital multimedia (1983), interactive video (1984), digital video and holography (1992), and Web-based portfolios (1995). He wrote *Communication Technology: Today and Tomorrow*, the first textbook to address digital cross-media publishing technologies (McGraw-Hill,

1991, 1996). He was founding editor of the *Journal of Technology Education* (*JTE*; 1989–1997) and pioneered free global access to the journal (beginning in 1992) before the Web became viable. He established and edited *Graphic Comm Central* (1997–2009), the Web portal for graphic communication educators. He began his career as a high school technology teacher in Albany, NY.

Mr. Michael Town
STEM High School

For the past 27 years Mike Town has taught numerous integrated STEM courses at the high school level in Redmond, Washington, including Advanced Placement environmental science and environmental engineering and sustainability design. The courses are dual credited and Career and Technical Education (CTE) certified. He has worked on committees to design standards for a state-certified CTE course in environmental science and sustainability and an endorsement certification in environmental and sustainability education for preservice teachers. He has also written environmental curriculum, most notably the Cool School Challenge (CSC), which enables students to conduct energy audits and develop action plans to measure and reduce the carbon footprint of schools across the United States. The CSC has won the EPA Clean Air Award, and Mike's students received the President's Environmental Youth Award from President Bush. Mike also helped design an environmental education center and serves as a board member for the Environmental Education Association of Washington. He has won the National Education Association Foundation Green Prize for the United States, Environmental Educator of the Year from the North American Association of Environmental Educators, and the Conservation Fund Environmental Educator Award for the United States. In 2010–2011, as a National Science Foundation Einstein Fellow, he worked on STEM education policy issues for the National Science Board. He also served on the steering committee for the NRC Board on Science Education workshop on Climate Change Education in the Formal Setting K–14 and is a current member of the NRC Teacher Advisory Committee. He earned degrees in environmental science and education from Huxley College of the Environment and Western Washington University and a master's degree in science education from the University of Washington.